TWO PLAYS BY ANN JELLICOE

 A DELTA BOOK 1964

THE KNACK

————and

THE SPORT OF MY MAD MOTHER

A Delta Book
Published by
Dell Publishing Co., Inc.
750 Third Avenue, New York, N.Y. 10017
Copyright © 1958, 1962 by Ann Jellicoe
Delta ® TM 755118, Dell Publishing Co., Inc.

Reprinted by arrangement with Faber and Faber Limited
24 Russell Square, London W.C. 1, England

All rights whatsoever in these plays are strictly reserved and
applications for performances in all countries should be made to
Margaret Ramsay Ltd., 14 Goodwin's Court, London, W.C. 2, England.
No performance of the play may be given unless a licence
has been obtained prior to rehearsal.

Library of Congress Catalog Card Number: 64-23978
First printing—November, 1964
Cover illustration by Moselle Thompson
Manufactured in the United States of America
Second Printing

THE KNACK

A Comedy

To
ROGER and KEITH

The first American production of *The Knack* was presented by The Establishment Theatre Company, Inc. on May 27, 1964, at The New Theatre, New York City, with the following cast:

Tom	Brian Bedford
Colin	Roddy Maude-Roxby
Tolen	George Segal
Nancy	Alexandra Berlin

Directed by Mike Nichols

This play was first presented by The English Stage Company at the Arts Theatre, Cambridge on 9th October 1961 with the following cast:

Tom	Terry Palmer
Colin	Ronald Falk
Tolen	David Sumner
Nancy	Rita Tushingham

Directed by Keith Johnstone
Designed by Alan Tagg

It was subsequently produced in London at the Royal Court Theatre on 27th March 1962 with the following cast:

Tom	James Bolam
Colin	Philip Locke
Tolen	Julian Glover
Nancy	Rita Tushingham

Directed by Ann Jellicoe and Keith Johnstone
Designed by Alan Tagg

CHARACTERS

TOM: Smallish in size. Vigorous, balanced, strong and sensitive in his movements. He speaks with a great range of pitch, pace and volume and with immense energy and vitality.

COLIN: Tall and uncoordinated. Explodes into speech and talks jerkily, flatly, haltingly. Basically a strong and intelligent man, but unsure of himself. Gets very angry with himself.

TOLEN: Once an unpromising physical specimen he has developed himself by systematic physical exercise. His body is now much as he would like it to be. He appears strong, well-built, full of rippling muscle. All his movements are a conscious display of this body. He almost always speaks with a level, clipped smoothness and a very considered subtlety of tone.

NANCY: Aged about seventeen. Potentially a beautiful girl but her personality, like her appearance, is still blurred and unformed. She wears an accordion-pleated skirt.

The acting area should be as close to the audience as possible.

10

ACT ONE

A room. The room is in the course of being painted by TOM. *The distribution of the paint is determined by the way the light falls. There is a window up left in the back wall and another down right. The paint is darkest where the shadows are darkest and light where they are most light. The painting is not smooth, pretty or finished, but fierce and determined. Onstage there is a step-ladder, a divan, two simple wooden chairs; a pair of chest expanders hangs from the door (down left).*
Curtain up. TOM *onstage. Enter* COLIN.

COLIN: Er . . . I . . . er . . .
TOM: Fabulous. It's fabulous. It's fantastic.
    (*Pause.*)
COLIN: Er . . .
TOM: Is it dry yet?
COLIN: Where?
TOM: Anywhere.
    (COLIN *tries.*)
COLIN: Getting on.
TOM: Good.
    (*Pause.*)
COLIN: I . . . er . . .
TOM: I hate that divan. (*Pause.*) More white there
    perhaps. More white. (*Pause.*) Here. How does
    the light fall?

11

COLIN: Eh?

TOM: The light. Get with it. White where it's light, black where it's dark, grey in between. (*Pause.*)

COLIN: Oh yes . . . yes.

TOM: Yes? Good. More white. (*He takes a brush of black paint and paints.*) Blast. (*He gets a rag, looks at wall, considers it and then starts working black paint with rag.*) Yes? Yes? (*Pause.*) Yes?

COLIN: It's not in the system.

TOM: Eh?

COLIN: White where it's light, black where it's dark.

TOM: It's nice. I like it.

COLIN: You're so messy. Everything's messed. It's so badly done.

TOM: I'm not, I'm not a decorator. It looks different, yes?

COLIN: Different?

TOM: Yes.

COLIN: To what?

TOM: To before I moved in. (*Pause.*) He won't like it.

COLIN: Who won't?

TOM: It'll annoy him. It'll annoy Tolen. It'll enrage him.

COLIN: The house doesn't belong to Tolen.

TOM: He'll say it's childish.

COLIN: It's my house. I rent it, so it's mine. (*Pause.*) There's a lot of stuff in the passage.

TOM: Ha ha! Because Tolen didn't think of it first.

COLIN: The passage is all bunged up. I want to bring my bed downstairs.

TOM: What's Tolen's first name?

COLIN: He says he hasn't got one.

TOM: Not got one?

12

COLIN: He never uses it. I want to bring my bed . . .

TOM: If he never uses it . . .

COLIN: . . . My bed downstairs.

TOM: He must have it.

COLIN: I want to bring my bed——

TOM: Well bring it down! What?

COLIN: I can't get it out of the front door.

TOM: You want to bring your bed——?

COLIN: There's too much stuff in the passage.

TOM: I put the stuff in the passage.

COLIN: There's a chest of drawers behind the front door. You can't get out.

TOM: Or in. Where's Tolen?

COLIN: Out. (*Pause.*) Seeing a girl.

TOM: Oh.

COLIN: There's too much stuff in the passage.

TOM: Why do you want to bring your bed downstairs?

COLIN: The wardrobe and the chest of drawers. We'll bring them in here.

TOM: What!

COLIN: Temporarily.

TOM: No.

COLIN: So I can get the bed through the front door.

TOM: We'll bring the bed in here and take it out through the window.
(*Slight pause.*)

COLIN: You only put the wardrobe outside while you were painting.

TOM: I don't want it back. The room's so beautiful.

COLIN: But you must be practical——

TOM: This blasted thing——

COLIN: You've got to sit——

TOM: The bottom's falling out.

COLIN: You've got to sleep——

13

TOM: Chairs!

COLIN: You can't sleep on the floor. Chairs?

TOM: On the floor. Sleep on it! I think I'll put the mattress on the floor!

COLIN: What!

TOM: Yes! The mattress on the floor. An empty—an empty beautiful room! What an angle! Look! Upwards? What an idea!
(COLIN *sinks bewildered on to a chair*.)
You marvel, you! (*Seizes* COLIN's *chair*.) On the wall! Out of the way! Off the floor! I'll hang them on the wall!

COLIN: Oh no!

TOM: Oh yes! (*Throws mattress on floor*.) Help! You! Come on! Help me! Help me! Colin! My God, what a splendid idea!

COLIN: There's too much stuff in the passage.

TOM: Put it in the basement.

COLIN: We haven't got a basement.

TOM: Give it to Tolen! Put it in Tolen's room! Yes! Come on, help me! Oh! A beautiful empty room! Why do you want to bring your bed downstairs?

COLIN: Getting another.

TOM: Oh?

COLIN: A bigger one. Six foot.
(*Pause*.)

TOM: Let's get this shifted.

COLIN: Hadn't we better bring mine in first?

TOM: Into the basement. Give it to Tolen.
(*Noise, (off), of motor-bike which shudders to a stop outside the front door.*)

COLIN: We haven't got a basement.

TOM: Tolen. That's his motor-bike.

14

(*Sound of somebody trying front door.*)

COLIN : It's Tolen. He can't get in. (*Shouting.*) Be with you.

(*Exit* TOM *and* COLIN *with divan. Enter* TOLEN *through window upstage.* COLIN *appears at window and disappears.*)

COLIN : (*off*). Not there.

TOM : (*off*). What?

COLIN : (*off*). He's disappeared.

TOM : (*off*). That's odd.

(*Enter* TOM *through door followed by* COLIN.)

COLIN : Oh there you . . .

TOLEN : Your windows are rather dirty.

TOM : Let's wash them.

COLIN : I—I've got some Windolene.

(*Exit* COLIN.)

TOM : What's that?

COLIN : (*off*). For cleaning windows.

(*Pause. Re-enter* COLIN *with Windolene which he hands to* TOM.)

TOM : (*reading label*). Wipe it on Windolene,
Wipe it off window clean.

(TOM *wipes some of the Windolene on the bottom half of the window.*)

TOLEN : Washing with clean water and then polishing with newspaper would have less electro-static action.

COLIN : Oh?

TOLEN : Would repel dirt more efficiently.

(TOM *starts to experiment with the various shapes he can make.*)

TOLEN : Now you must do the top half, Tom.

(TOM *hoists the bottom half of the window up and*

crosses to window D.R. *and puts on the Windolene there.*)

TOLEN: You do realize, Tom, that in order to clean the window, you have to wipe off the Windolene? (*Pause.*) The white stuff has to be polished off the window.

TOM: Let's get that bed down, shall we, Colin?

COLIN: You can't leave that stuff on.

TOM: Oh?

TOLEN: You can't leave it on. "Wipe on sparingly with a damp cloth and wipe off immediately."

TOM: It's as good as net curtains, only better.

COLIN: Net curtains?

TOM: You should paint your windows white, Tolen. White reflects heat. You'll be O.K. when the bomb drops.
(*Exit* TOM.)

COLIN: What? What did you say?

TOM: (*off*). O.K. when the bomb drops. O.K. when the . . .

COLIN: Net curtains?
(*Exit* COLIN. *Pause.* TOLEN *is about to exit when he hears bumps, crashes and yells, off. This resolves into dialogue*):

COLIN: (*off*). It won't go round.

TOM: (*off*). It will.

COLIN: (*off*). It won't. Take it apart.

TOM: (*off*). What?

COLIN: (*off*). Take it to bits.

TOM: (*off*). Oh, all right.

COLIN: (*off*). Can you take the head?

TOM: (*off*). The what?

COLIN: (*off*). The head! Hold the head! The head!

TOM: (*off*). Help!

16

COLIN: (*off*). Eh?

TOM: (*off*). Help! Help!

COLIN: (*off*). Mind the plaster. (*Crash* (*off*).) Oh!

TOM: (*off*). You're so houseproud.

(*Enter* COLIN *with head of bed.* COLIN *is about to lean head against wall.*)

Not where it's wet! Fool!

(COLIN *leans head against step-ladder. Crash* (*off*).)

Help! Help! I'm stuck! (*Laughing.*) I'm stuck! The foot!

COLIN: The what?

TOM: (*off*). The foot!

COLIN: Your foot!

(*Exit* COLIN.)

TOM: (*off*). Of the bed.

(*Banging and crashing* (*off*) *with various imprecations. Enter* COLIN *with foot of bed.*)

TOLEN: Have there been any telephone calls?

COLIN: Eh?

TOLEN: I'm expecting a couple of girls to telephone.

COLIN: There was a Maureen and er—a Joan.

TOLEN: Joan? Joan who?

(COLIN *is nonplussed.*)

Never mind, she'll telephone again. (*Pause.*) I was afraid it was the barmaid at the "Sun".

COLIN: Alice?

(*Enter* TOM.)

TOLEN: She took me into the little back room this morning.

TOM: What about Jimmy?

TOLEN: Probably at Chapel.

TOM: On Saturday?

TOLEN: She said he was at Chapel. Beyond that bead

17

curtain you know, there's a room full of silver cups. Cases of them. And a large pink sofa in the middle. I never knew Jimmy was a sporting man.

COLIN : Who was the other one?

TOLEN : The other?

COLIN : The one you were expecting to telephone.

TOLEN : Girl I met in a telephone kiosk.
(*Exit* TOLEN. *Small crash* (*off*). *Re-enter* TOLEN.)

TOLEN : Colin, would you mind moving that bed? I would like to get up to my room.

COLIN : Oh, the base. Sorry.

TOM : Can't you climb over?
(*Exit* COLIN. *Crashing sounds* (*off*). *Re-enter* COLIN.)

COLIN : (*to* TOM). Give me a hand, will you?

TOM : Why can't Tolen?

COLIN : Eh?

TOM : It's him that wants to get upstairs.

COLIN : Oh, er . . .
(*Exit* COLIN. *Re-enter dragging base.*)

TOM : Mind the paint.
(TOM *helps* COLIN *onstage with bed.*)

TOLEN : Why are you bringing your bed downstairs, Colin?

COLIN : Getting a new one.

TOLEN : Oh?

COLIN : A bigger one—six foot.

TOLEN : Oh, like mine.

COLIN : I—er—I thought—I thought I'd like another one. You know—er—bigger. Just—just in case, you know. I thought I'd like a bigger—another bed—more comfortable. (*Pause.*) I could always put my married cousins up.

18

(*Long pause.*)

TOLEN: Have you got a girl yet, Colin?

COLIN: No.

TOLEN: Carol left six months ago, didn't she?

COLIN: Mm.

TOM: Have you got a girl yet, Colin?

COLIN: No.

TOM: Got a woman?

COLIN: No.

TOM: You haven't, have you.

COLIN: No.

TOM: You haven't!

COLIN: No.

TOM: You haven't! You haven't! You fool! Why d'you want another bed?

COLIN: Mind my bed!

TOM: His bed! Colin's bed!

COLIN: It's not strong.

TOM: (*through the bars*). Grr! Grr!

COLIN: Hey! Stop! Stop it!

TOM: It creaks! It runs! It spins! Watch it! Yahoo!

COLIN: You'll——

TOM: Poop—poop——

COLIN: I say——

TOM: Poop poop poop poop——

COLIN: Stop it. Stop it.

TOM: Poop poop, look out!

COLIN: Stop stop—ow!
(*Everything collapses.* TOM *and* COLIN *are enmeshed in the bed and step-ladder.*)

COLIN: You—you—you nit.
(*Pause.*)

TOLEN: Did you put turpentine in the white?

TOM: Eh?

TOLEN : The white paint. Did you put turpentine in the white?

TOM : Yes.

TOLEN : It'll go yellow.

COLIN : What?

TOLEN : The white paint will go yellow.

COLIN : Yellow!

TOLEN : Yes.

COLIN : I never knew that.

TOLEN : The turpentine thins the white lead in the paint and the linseed oil seeps through and turns the white yellow.

COLIN : Oh. D'you think we should do it again?

(TOM *is pulling at the chest expanders.*)

TOM : Peter left these, wasn't it nice of him?

(*Pause. A girl passes the window.* TOLEN *starts to exit through window.*)

COLIN : Where are you going? Where——

(*Exit* TOLEN.)

How does he do it?

TOM : He's beginning to wear out my window. Let's move the chest of drawers so he can come in through the front door. He doesn't actually do them in the street, you know.

COLIN : Doesn't he?

TOM : He makes his contact and stashes them up for later. He's enlarging his collection.

COLIN : How does he meet them?

TOM : Your bed's in the way. What are we going to do with this bed? What you going to do with it?

COLIN : Oh that. Oh—what's the use?

(TOM *lugs part of the bed across and leans it against* COLIN.)

20

What's Tolen got that I haven't got? **Maureen**
says Tolen's got sexy ankles.
(TOM *brings up another piece and leans it against*
COLIN.)
Are my ankles sexy?

TOM: What are you going to do with this bed?

COLIN: Thought I'd take it round to Copp Street.

TOM: Copp Street?

COLIN: To the junk yard.

TOM: To sell?

COLIN: I thought so.

TOM: For money?

COLIN: Why not?

TOM: O.K. We'll take it round to
Copp Street. How far is it to Copp Street?

COLIN: Twenty minutes.

TOM: Twenty! (*Long pause.*) Put it back in your room.
(*Pause.* COLIN *shakes his head. Pause.* TOM *opens
his mouth to speak.*)

COLIN: (*interrupting*). Not in the passage.
(*Pause.*)

TOM: Can't you just stand there? You look quite nice
really.
(*Slight pause.*)

COLIN: Put it together.

TOM: No.

COLIN: If we put it together it'll stand by itself.

TOM: No.

COLIN: On its own feet.

TOM: I can't bear it.
(*Pause.*)

COLIN: Take the foot.
(TOM *does so listlessly.*)

And the head.

(TOM *does so*.)

TOM: How can you sleep on this? I'd think I was at the zoo.

COLIN: How d'you get a woman? How can I get a girl?

(*They start to put the bed together*.)

TOM: Do you know why the Duck-billed Platypus can't be exported from Australia—or do I mean platipi?

COLIN: How can I get a woman?

TOM: You think this is going to be a silly story, don't you.

COLIN: Well?

TOM: Because they eat their own weight in worms every day and they starve to death in one and a half hours or something. It's rather a nice object. It's not a nice bed but it's not a bad object. Yes. Look. It's rather nice.

(COLIN *picks up mattress*.)

No.

COLIN: But——

TOM: No.

COLIN: But a mattress naturally goes on a bed.

TOM: It's not a bed. It's an object. More than that, it's wheeled traffic. Mm. Not much room, is there? I must get those chairs off the floor. Put the mattress in the passage.

COLIN: It's more comfy on the bed.

TOM: Oh, very well.

(TOM *experiments with the bed*.)

COLIN: Why is Tolen so sexy?

(TOLEN *passes the window and tries the front door. Enters by window*.)

TOM: You were very quick. Did she repulse you?

22

TOLEN: No. I'm seeing her later.

TOM: Next time I'll time you.

TOLEN: Next time come and watch me.

(TOM *takes the chest expanders and tries them a few times.*)

TOM: I'm getting pretty good. Whew! I can do ten of these. Whew! It's awful!

TOLEN: I can do twenty—but then . . .

TOM: Let's see you.

(TOLEN *indicates he is below bothering to use his energy.*)

COLIN: I can do twenty as well.

TOM: Let's see you.

(COLIN *takes the chest expanders and starts.*)

He's bending his elbows, it's easier that way.

COLIN: Four.

TOM: Tolen.

TOLEN: Yes, Tom?

TOM: Do you think it's a good idea for Colin to buy a six-foot bed?

TOLEN: Where's he buying it?

COLIN: Nine. (*Pause.*) Catesby's.

TOM: Plutocrat.

TOLEN: Heal's would have been better.

COLIN: Twelve. Eh?

TOLEN: Heal's have more experience with beds.

COLIN: Expensive. Fourteen.

TOLEN: They may be more expensive, but they have more experience. You pay for their greater experience.

TOM: Yes, but do you think it's a good idea, a sound idea, ethically, for Colin to buy a six-foot bed when he hasn't got a woman?

TOLEN: Rory McBride has an eight-foot bed.

23

TOM : Don't stop! You have to keep it up the whole time. You're not allowed to stop. How sexy is Rory McBride? Who is he anyway?

COLIN : D'you think——?

TOM : Don't stop!

COLIN : D'you think——?

TOM : What?

COLIN : I ought to get an eight-foot bed?
(COLIN *stops*.)

TOM : How many?

COLIN : Twenty-four. (*Staggering*.) Where's the bed?

TOM : You mean the object.
(COLIN *collapses on the bed. A girl is seen to pass the window. Exit* TOLEN *through window*.)

COLIN : Where's he gone?

TOM : A girl passed by and he went after her.
(*Pause*.)

COLIN : You got a cigarette?

TOM : I thought you didn't smoke.

COLIN : Have you got a cigarette?

TOM : No. (*Pause*.) Listen, Colin, I've had a new idea for you. For teaching children about music.

COLIN : Oh——

TOM : Listen! My idea about the chalk—was it a good one?

COLIN : It was all right.

TOM : Did you use it or not? Did you?

COLIN : All right. All right. Just tell me.

TOM : Tolen could help, blast him.

COLIN : How?

TOM : He's a musician. You need his advice. But don't let that bastard near the kids, he'll bully them. Now listen, I been thinking about this. You got a piano? Well, have you? Golly the bleeding

24

school wouldn't be furnished without a piano.

COLIN: We've got one.

TOM: Good. Listen, I been thinking about this. Teaching's so intellectual and when it's not intellectual, it's bossy, or most of it. The teachers tell the kids everything and all they get is dull little copycats, little automata; dim, limited and safe——

COLIN: Oh, get on.

TOM: You get the piano and you get the kids and you say it's a game see? "Right," you say, "You're not to look at the keys, 'cos that's cheating."

COLIN: Not look——

TOM: If they look at each other playing, they'll just copy each other. Now, don't put your own brain between them and the direct experience. Don't intellectualize. Let them come right up against it. And don't talk about music, talk about noise.

COLIN: Noi——

TOM: What else is music but an arrangement of noises? I'm serious. "Now," you say, "one of you come out here and make noises on the piano." And finally one of them will come out and sort of hit the keys, bang, bang. "Right," you say, "now someone come out and make the same noise."

COLIN: Eh?

TOM: The same noise. That's the first step. They'll have to *listen* to see they hit in the same place— and they can do it more or less 'cos they can sort of—you know—clout it in the middle bit. So next you get them all going round the piano in a circle, all making the same noise, and they'll love that. When they get a bit cheesed, you develop it. "O.K.," you say, "let's have another noise."

COLIN: I don't see the point, I mean——

TOM: Now listen, this way they'll find out for themselves, give them a direct experience and they'll discover for themselves—all the basic principles of music and they won't shy away—they won't think of it as culture, it'll be pop to them. Listen! You, goon, moron, you don't like Bartok, do you?

COLIN: No.

TOM: Don't be so pleased with yourself. You don't understand it, your ear's full of Bach, it stops at Mahler. But after a few lessons like this, you play those kids Schoenberg, you play them Bartok. They'll know what he's doing. I bet they will! It'll be rock'n roll to them. My God, I ought to be a teacher! My God I'm a genius!

COLIN: What about Tolen?

TOM: What about him?

COLIN: You said he could help.

TOM: To borrow his gramophone records.

COLIN: He never lends them, he never lets anyone else touch them. (*Pause.*) It's a good idea.

TOM: Good.

COLIN: Thanks. (*Pause.*) Why do you say Tolen is a bastard?

TOM: Be careful. He only dazzles you for one reason. Really, Colin, sex, sex, sex: that's all we ever get from you.

COLIN: It's all right for you and Tolen.

TOM: We're all of us more or less total sexual failures.

26

COLIN: Tolen isn't a sexual failure.

TOM: He needs it five hours a day, he says.

COLIN: Then he can't be a sexual failure. (*Pause.*) He can't be a sexual failure. (*Pause.*) He can't be a sexual failure having it five hours a day. (*Pause.*) Can he?

(*Long pause.*)

TOM: I don't like that wall. There's something wrong with that wall. It's not right.

COLIN: Can he?

(NANCY *appears outside behind the window up left and looks about her.*)

TOM: Hm. Colin——

COLIN: Can he?

TOM: Colin.

(NANCY *vanishes.*)

COLIN: What?

TOM: Oh nothing. What do you think about that wall?

COLIN: Blast the wall! Blast the bloody wall!

(NANCY *reappears outside the window.*)

Oh . . . oh . . . oh . . .

TOM: Speak to her.

COLIN: I—I——

TOM: Ask her the time. Ask her to lend you sixpence.

COLIN: I—I—you.

TOM: Eh?

COLIN: You—please.

TOM: I can't do it for you.

COLIN: Oh——

(COLIN *turns away. Pause.* NANCY *vanishes. Long pause.*)

27

TOM : What do you think about that wall?

COLIN : What? Oh . . . it's . . . it's . . .

(COLIN *does something violent. Pause. Enter*
TOLEN *through window.*)

TOM : Someone was riding your motor-bike.

TOLEN : What?

(*Exit* TOLEN *through window.*)

COLIN : Who was riding his motor-bike?

(*Re-enter* TOLEN *through window.*)

TOM : I swear someone was riding your motor-bike.
(*Pause.*) Well?

TOLEN : Well?

TOM : How long did you take this time?

TOLEN : Did you time me?

TOM : Did you time yourself?

COLIN : How long did you take?

TOLEN : Not more than about ten minutes——

COLIN : Ten minutes! Only ten minutes!

TOLEN : Really, Colin, do you think I'm so clumsy, so
vulgar as to do it in the street? I'm meeting
her . . .

TOM : Ten minutes! Ten minutes from door to door?
From start to finish? From hello to good-bye?

COLIN : Ten minutes.

TOM : Ten Tolen! Ten! Ten minutes! Ten whole
minutes! What! No! You're slipping, man!
You're sliding! You're letting us down! Ten.
You can do better than that. Faster man!
Faster! Faster! Faster!

COLIN : Eh?

TOM : Give him a drink of water. Listen, Tolen. Three!
Three! Three! D'you hear? Dreams I got for
you, Tolen. Dreams and plans I got for you.
Four minutes! Get it down to four minutes.

Four minutes from start to finish—like the
four-minute mile.

COLIN: Eh?

TOM: Heroic! Think! A new series in the Olympic
Games!

COLIN: Is he joking?

TOM: And then, Tolen, by discipline, by training, by
application: three minutes fifty-nine seconds!
Three minutes fifty-five! Three minutes fifty!
And then—one day—one unimaginable day:
three minutes! Three minutes from start to
finish!

COLIN: Is it nicer, faster?

TOM: Nice? Nice? Nice? That's not the point. My
God! I'm disappointed in you, Tolen, My God
I am! Yes! I am! A man with every advantage,
every opportunity, every accoutrement—God's
gift to woman! And think of those women
Tolen: waiting to be satisfied—their need,
Tolen, their crying need—(*weeping.*) And with
the capacity, with the capacity for, with the
capacity for spreading yourself around.
(*Pause while* TOM *regains control.*)

TOLEN: I think you're mad.

TOM: Ah, Tolen, never mind. Relax. I see what you
mean. I'm a man too. I understand. Yes, I do.
Yes, yes I do. (*Slight pause.*) You couldn't do it.
(*Slight pause.*) You couldn't keep it up. You
couldn't keep up the pace.
(TOLEN *appears slightly restive.*)
Nobody could. It's too much. It's too fast. It's
not human, it's superhuman. No, no, let's forget
it. Let's be generous. I understand. (*Pause.*)
Wait! Here's what I propose. Here's what I

29

suggest. One in three! One in three in your own time! Yes Tolen, every third one as long as you like.

(TOLEN *yawns and climbs on the bed*.)

He's tired. He's weary. He's overdone it. Poor chap. He's tired. Poor bloke. Quick, quick. Blankets! Brandy! Pills! Pillows! Nurses! Stretchers! Doses! Nurses! Horlicks! Nurses! Hot water bottles! Nurses! Nurses! Nurses! Nurses! Have a piece of barley sugar.

(NANCY *appears at window*. TOLEN *takes notice*. NANCY *disappears*.)

Save yourself! Control yourself! Give yourself a chance!

TOLEN: A bit too provincial.

COLIN: What?

TOLEN: That girl.

(*Pause*.)

TOM: (*really wanting to know*). How can you tell she's provincial?

TOLEN: Of course, Tom, you will not appreciate that the whole skill, the whole science, is in the slowness: the length of time a man may take. The skill is in the slowness. Of course, Tom, I don't expect you can appreciate this. There is little skill, Tom, and no subtlety in the three-minute make. However——

COLIN: It's better slower?

TOLEN: However, if I wished, Tom, if I wanted, you do realize that I could do it in about eighty-five seconds.

TOM: Yes.

COLIN: Tolen.

TOLEN: Yes, Colin?

30

COLIN: Will you—I mean—will you show me— (*pause*) how— (*pause*)?

TOLEN: You mean how I get women?

COLIN: Yes.

TOLEN: I can tell you what I know intellectually, Colin, what my experience has been. But beyond that it's a question of intuition. Intuition is, to some degree, inborn, Colin. One is born with an intuition as to how to get women. But this feeling can be developed with experience and confidence, in certain people, Colin, to some degree. A man can develop the knack.

First you must realize that women are not individuals but types. No, not even types, just women. They want to surrender but they don't want the responsibility of surrendering. This is one reason why the man must dominate.

On the other hand there are no set rules. A man must be infinitely subtle; must use his intuition, a very subtle intuition. If you feel it necessary in order to get the woman you must even be prepared to humiliate yourself, to grovel, to utterly abase yourself before the woman—I mean only in cases of extreme necessity, Colin. After all, what does it matter? It's just part of getting her. Once you've got her it's the woman that grovels. Finally, Colin, the man is the master.

For you must appreciate, Colin, that people like to be dominated. They like to be mastered. They ask to be relieved of the responsibility of deciding for themselves. It's a kindness towards people to relieve them of responsibility. In this

31

world, Colin, there are the masters and there are the servants. Very few men are real men, Colin, are real masters. Almost all women are servants. They don't want to think for themselves, they want to be dominated.

First you must establish contact. Of course you won't find that as easy as I do. I'm not referring to touch, tactile communication, that comes later. I mean the feeling between you. You are aware of the girl, the girl is aware of you, a vibration between you . . .

COLIN: Just a minute.

TOLEN: Yes?

COLIN: I just want to get it straight.

TOLEN: Take your time.

(*Pause.*)

COLIN: I don't see what you mean by contact.

TOLEN: Very difficult to explain. Tom, can you explain?

TOM: No.

TOLEN: Once you feel it, Colin, you will know it next time. Having established this basis of contact, then you work to break down her resistance, to encourage surrender. Flattery is useful; if a woman is intelligent make her think she's pretty, if she's pretty make her think she's beautiful. Never let them think, never let them see you are clever or intellectual. Never be serious with a woman. Once you let a woman start thinking, the whole process takes infinitely more time. Keep her laughing, keep her talking; you can judge by her laughter, by the way she laughs, how you're getting on.

Perhaps it might be useful to consider what is the right food.

COLIN: The right food?

TOLEN: Food is of the utmost importance. Food is of the essence. One's body needs protein and energy-giving substance. I find with my perhaps unusual sexual demands that my body requires at least twice the normal daily intake of protein.

COLIN: Protein?

TOLEN: Cheese, eggs, milk, meat. I drink about four pints of milk a day—Channel Island milk. And eat about a pound of steak. It needn't be the most expensive, the cheaper cuts have the same food value. For instance, skirt.

TOM: Skirt?

TOLEN: Skirt.

COLIN: Skirt. Cheese, eggs, milk, meat, skirt. Got a pencil, Tom.

TOLEN: Skirt is meat.

COLIN: Oh.

TOM: Don't you see what you're doing to this growing lad? He hasn't got a woman, now he'll go and eat himself silly on milk and meat. Stoke up the fire and block up the chimney. Listen, Colin, suppose this was a piano.

TOLEN: A what?

COLIN: Shut up.

TOM: A piano. Plonk, plonk, plonk.

TOLEN: It's a bed.

TOM: It's not, it's a piano, listen.

COLIN: I want Tolen to tell me——

TOM: Shut up, he's told you enough. A piano, plonk. Now supposing you couldn't——

COLIN: Listen, Tolen——

TOM: Supposing you couldn't see my hand——

COLIN: Shut up.

33

TOM: I play—C sharp, F and A——
COLIN: Tolen——
(NANCY *passes window*.)
I want—listen to me. I want to hear what—I
want to hear what Tolen has to say. Listen—
listen to me. I want to hear wh-what Tolen has
to say. So *what* you think it's b-bad for me to
listen to Tolen. You're not in charge of me. I
am and I'm sick of myself, I'm absolutely sick,
and here I am stuck with myself. I want to hear
what Tolen has to say——
(NANCY *reappears at window*.)
I want to hear what Tolen has to say. So *what* I
want to hear, I want to hear what——
(NANCY *taps at window. Pause*.)
NANCY: Do you know where I can find the Y.W.C.A.?
(*Pause*.)
TOM: The what?
NANCY: The Y.W.C.A.
(*Pause*.)
TOM: Come on in. Come in by the front door.
(*Exit* TOM.)
NANCY: Oh thanks. Thanks very much.
(*Sound of weighty object being moved. Enter*
NANCY *carrying a holdall and a carrier bag and*
TOM *carrying a large suitcase*.)
NANCY: Hullo.
TOLEN: Hullo.
NANCY: Hullo.
COLIN: Oh, hullo.
(*Pause*.)
TOM: Well, has anyone seen it?
COLIN: Seen what?
TOM: Seen what?

34

NANCY: The Y.W.C.A.

TOM: The Y.W.C.A.

COLIN: Oh, the Y.W.C.A.

TOM: Yes.

COLIN: No.

(*Pause.*)

TOM: Would you like to sit down?

NANCY: Well, thanks, but—but well, thanks.

(*She sits.*)

TOM: Would you like a cup of tea or something?

NANCY: Oh, well, no thanks, really.

TOM: No trouble, it's no trouble. I'll put the kettle on

(*Exit* TOM.)

TOLEN: Did he say he'd put a kettle on? He's not boiled
a kettle since he came here.

TOM: (*off*). Colin!

COLIN: Yes?

TOM: (*off*). How do you turn the gas on?

(*Pause.* TOLEN *now pursues the intention of
teasing* NANCY *and making her uncomfortable.
He succeeds. If possible achieve this without
words. But if necessary insert line:*

TOLEN: *"Bit short in the neck. Nice hair though."*
Enter TOM.)

TOM: How do you turn— (*pause.*) What do you think
of our piano?

NANCY: What?

TOM: Our piano: Do you like it? Our piano?

NANCY: What piano?

TOM: This piano.

NANCY: Piano?

TOM: Yes.

NANCY: That's not a piano.

TOM: Yes it is, it's a piano.

35

NANCY: It's a bed.

TOM: It's a piano, honest, listen: ping!

NANCY: It's a bed.

TOM: It's a piano, isn't it, Colin?

COLIN: Eh?

TOM: This is a piano.

COLIN: Piano?

TOM: Piano.

COLIN: Oh yes, a piano. Ping.

NANCY: It's a bed.

TOM: (*using the edge of the bed as keyboard*). Ping (*high*) ping (*low*). Ping (*running his finger right down: glissando*) pi-i-i-i-i-ng.

COLIN: (*middle*). Ping.

NANCY: It's a bed.

TOM: Bechstein.

NANCY: Bechstein?

TOM: (*high*) ping. (*Medium high*) ping. (*Medium low*) ping. (*Low*) ping.

NANCY: It's a bed.

TOM: (*1st 3 bars "Blue Danube" starting low*).
Ping ping ping ping ping.

NANCY: It's a bed.

COLIN: Rosewood.

TOM: (*4th and 5th bars B.D.*).
Ping ping
Ping ping.

NANCY: It's a bed.

TOM: (*6th, 7th, 8th bars B.D.*).
Ping ping ping ping ping
Ping ping.

COLIN: (*taking over 9th bar*). Ping ping.

TOM, COLIN: (*together playing chords in unison 10th–13th bars*).

36

Ping ping ping ping ping
Ping ping
Ping ping
Ping ping ping ping ping
Ping ping.

NANCY: (*tentative, taking over*). Ping ping.

TOM, COLIN: (*gently encouraging* NANCY *who joins in
17th, 18th, 19th bars B.D.*).
Ping ping ping ping ping
Ping ping
Ping ping.
(*All three letting go with great rich chords.*)
Ping ping ping ping ping
Ping ping
Ping ping
Ping ping ping ping ping
Ping ping ping ping
Ping ping ping ping ping ping.

NANCY: Ping.
COLIN: Ping.
NANCY: Ping.
COLIN: Ping.
NANCY: Ping.
COLIN: Plong.
NANCY: Plong.
COLIN: Plong plong.
NANCY: Ping plong.
COLIN: Plong.
NANCY: Ping.
COLIN: Ping.
NANCY: Plong.
(*Pause.*)
COLIN: Plong.
(*Pause.*)

37

NANCY: Plong.
  (*Pause.*)
COLIN: Plong.
TOLEN: Why be so childish about a bed?

> *Author's Note:* All the above could be rearranged or
> improvised to suit different actors and different pro-
> ductions provided the sequence of events is clear:
> 1. TOM and COLIN charm NANCY into entering into the
> game.
> 2. TOM retires leaving COLIN and NANCY getting on
> rather well, a growing relationship which TOLEN
> interrupts.

  (*Long pause.*)
TOM: Would anyone like to know how they train
  lions to stand on boxes? (*Pause.*) Would you
  like to know how they train lions to stand on
  boxes? First we must have a box (*taking bucket*)
  That will do. Now this marks the limit of the
  cage—the edge, the bars.
TOLEN: Must you be so childish?
TOM: Childlike. The trainer takes his whip. Whip?
  Whip? We'll do without a whip. Now a lion. I
  must have a lion . . . Tolen, you'd make a good
  lion. No? O.K. Colin.
COLIN: No.
TOM: Come on, be a lion.
COLIN: No.
TOM: Go on, can't you roar? The trainer taking the
  box in his left hand, and the whip—imagine the
  whip—in his right, advances on the lion and
  drives him backward against the cage bars, yes?
  Now. There is a critical moment when the lion
  must leap at the attacker otherwise it will be too

38

late, see? Right. The trainer can recognize the critical moment. So, at the moment when the lion rears to attack, the trainer draws back and the lion, no longer threatened, drops his forepaws and finds himself standing on the box. Do this a few times and you've trained a lion to stand on a box.

(*Pause.*)

COLIN: How does the box get there?

TOM: What?

COLIN: You've still got it in your hand.

TOM: The trainer puts it there.

COLIN: When?

(*Pause.*)

TOM: Let's try. You come and be lion.

COLIN: No.

TOM: All right, I'll be lion. (*He tries a roar or two.*) Whew! It makes you feel sexy. (*He tries again.*)

COLIN: I'd like to be lion.

TOM: All right.

COLIN: I wonder if I could roar into something.

TOM: Eh?

COLIN: It would help the resonance. (*He roars into bucket.*)

TOM: That's the lion's box.

COLIN: Sounds marvellous inside.

(COLIN *sees* NANCY's *carrier bag. He picks it up.*)

TOM: Hey, you can't touch that.

COLIN: Eh?

NANCY: Oh, that's all right.

(COLIN *empties contents, including a copy of* Honey *magazine. Puts carrier bag on his head and goes round roaring.*)

TOM: Yes! Yes! Yes! Yes! Yes!

(COLIN *roars at* TOM *who roars back, then at* NANCY. NANCY *laughs, half scared, half excited.* COLIN *roars at her and she runs away.* COLIN *gropes around for her, but she evades him, laughing.*)

TOM: You should wear a carrier bag more often.

COLIN: Just a minute.

(COLIN *takes the bag off his head and makes holes for eyes. Replaces bag. Roars again after* NANCY. TOLEN *takes off belt he wears and cracks it like a whip.*)

TOLEN: I'll be trainer.

TOM: Eh? Very well.

TOLEN: Ready?

(*Pause.* TOLEN *advances on* COLIN *cracking his "whip" and getting a sweet pleasure from the identification.* COLIN *roars,* TOLEN *gets more excited.*)

TOLEN: Back—back you—back you—back—back you beast you—beast you beast you back back!

(NANCY *gets mixed up between them. She screams and exits.* TOLEN *picks up* Honey. *Pause.*)

TOM: Just think what you could do with a real whip, Tolen. Or a Sjambok. Think of that.

COLIN: (*taking off carrier bag*). What's happened? Has she gone?

TOM: She left her suitcases.

(*End of Act One*)

40

ACT TWO

The room is very peaceful. TOM *is painting gently and thinking about his paint.* COLIN *has the carrier bag on his head and is feeling free and experimental. Anything the actor may improvise is probably best, but* COLIN *might feel like some exotic bird: standing on one leg, hopping, crowing; possibly using the chest expanders in some unconventional way. After a long pause.*

TOM : What do you think?
  (*Pause.*)
COLIN : Not thinking.
  (*Pause.*)
TOM : Eh?
  (*Pause.*)
COLIN : Not thinking.
TOM : Look!
COLIN : Oh.
TOM : A . . . (*pause*). This place soothes me.
  (*Pause.* COLIN *takes off the carrier bag.*)
COLIN : I remember the first time I saw this street.
TOM : Northam Street?
COLIN : These mean streets (*pause*)—the feeling of space in these streets—it's fantastic. (*Pause.*) When they're empty they're sort of—splendid, a sort of—crumbling splendour (*pause*) and a feeling of—in winter, on a hazy, winter day a—a—a

41

——romantic! And in summer hot and—listless.
And at week-ends, summer and the sun shining
and children dashing about and mothers talking
—you know, gossiping and men cleaning motor-
bikes and (*getting excited*) they can be forbid-
ding, threatening—I mean—you know—if the
light's flat and darkish,—no sun—just flat and
lowering, it's stupendous! And early morning—
early autumn—I've walked through these streets
all alone, you know, all by myself—so quiet
so . . . so . . .
(*Telephone rings* (*off*).)
It'll be for him. It'll be for Tolen.
(COLIN *replaces carrier bag on his head and picks
up a magazine. Exit* TOM. *Telephone stops
ringing. Pause.* NANCY *appears at the window, she
doesn't see* COLIN. NANCY *climbs through the
window and goes towards the suitcases.* COLIN
sees NANCY. NANCY *sees* COLIN *and is transfixed.
Pause. Enter* TOLEN *through window. Pause.*
TOLEN *whips off his belt.* NANCY *darts away
hysterical. There is a maelstrom of movement
during which the bed gets overturned,* NANCY *is
caught behind it and* COLIN *and* TOLEN *are
covering all the exits. Enter* TOM *through door.
Pause.*)

TOM : Colin, take that carrier bag off your head.
COLIN : Eh?
TOM : Take it off.
(COLIN *removes carrier bag.*)
Shall we get the bed straight? (TOM *goes to the
foot of the bed.*) Tolen?
(TOM *and* COLIN *put bed right.*)
You not found the Y.W.C.A.?

42

NANCY: No.

TOM: What's the address?

NANCY: I've got it here. (*She hands him a scrap of paper.*)

TOM: Martin's Grove W.2. Where's Martin's Grove?

COLIN: I don't know. I'll get the street map.

(*Exit* COLIN. *Pause.*)

NANCY: Thanks.

TOLEN: That's all right.

NANCY: Oh, thanks.

TOLEN: Don't mention it.

(*Enter* COLIN *with map.*)

TOM: How does it work?

COLIN: Index.

TOM: Eh?

COLIN: Back.

TOM: I see.

TOLEN: Just come off the train, have you?

NANCY: Yes.

COLIN: James Park, James Square, turn over, and again. Ah. Mapperton, Marlow.

TOLEN: Is it the——

TOM: Martin's Grove W.2. J4.73. What's that?

COLIN: Page seventy-three.

TOLEN: Is it the first time you've been here?

NANCY: Here?

TOLEN: In London?

NANCY: Oh yes.

(TOLEN *and* NANCY *laugh.*)

COLIN: Square J above, 4 across.

TOM: What tiny print.

TOLEN: You've got Chinese eyebrows.

NANCY: Eh?

TOLEN: Chinese eyebrows. Very clear arch. Very delicate.

NANCY: Have I?

43

TOLEN: Have you got a mirror, I'll show you.

NANCY: Oh.

COLIN: Turn it the other way.

TOM: Eh?

COLIN: Round. That's it.

TOLEN: See? Very pretty.

NANCY: Oh.

TOM: Here. (*Pause.*) Here it is.

NANCY: Eh? Oh, thanks.

TOM: Not far. Five minutes. (NANCY *is occupied with* TOLEN.) We'll take you. We'll take you there.

NANCY: Oh. Oh thanks. (*Pause.*) Well perhaps I ought to——

TOLEN: What's your name?

NANCY: Nancy, Nancy Jones. What's yours?

TOLEN: Tolen.

NANCY: Tolen? Tolen what?

TOLEN: Tolen.

NANCY: Tolen, oh I see, like Capucine.

TOLEN: I beg your pardon?

NANCY: Capucine.

TOLEN: Capucine?

NANCY: Like Capucine. Nothing Capucine, Capucine nothing.

TOLEN: Please would you tell me what you mean?

NANCY: You not seen her? She's an actress. She acts.

TOLEN: On television?

NANCY: In the films.   Is it your christian name or your surname? (*Pause.*) Well, is it? Is it your surname or your christian name?

TOLEN: It's my surname.

NANCY: What's your christian name?

TOLEN: I never use my first name. I have no first name.

NANCY: What is it?

TOLEN: I prefer not to use it.

44

NANCY: Why?

TOLEN: I don't use it. I have no first name. I never use my first name.

(TOLEN *moves away. Pause.* TOLEN *returns to near* NANCY. NANCY *shifts uncomfortably.*)

What's the matter? Is anything wrong? Is anything the matter with you?

NANCY: No.

TOLEN: Why are you so nervous?

NANCY: I'm not.

TOLEN: You look nervous.

NANCY: Me nervous? Do I?

TOLEN: Yes.

NANCY: Oh——

TOLEN: Yes?

NANCY: Nothing.

TOLEN: What's the matter?

NANCY: It's—it's——

TOLEN: Well?

NANCY: It's——

TOLEN: You are nervous, aren't you? Very nervous. Why don't you take your coat off?

NANCY: I don't want to.

TOLEN: My dear, you take it off.

NANCY: I don't want to.

TOLEN: Why don't you want to?

NANCY: No.

(*Exit* COLIN.)

It's—it's——

TOLEN: Yes?

(*Pause.*)

NANCY: You're looking at me.

TOLEN: Am I?

NANCY: Yes.

45

TOLEN: How am I looking?

NANCY: I don't know, I——

TOLEN: How am I looking?

NANCY: I——

TOLEN: Well?

NANCY: I feel——

TOLEN: What?

NANCY: I don't know, I——

TOLEN: You feel funny, don't you—go on, tell me—go on—tell me—tell me.

(NANCY *moves away.* TOLEN *laughs.*)

TOM: What's the most frightening building in London?

TOLEN: It depends what you mean by frightening.

TOM: Break it up, Tolen.

TOLEN: What I do is my affair, not yours.

TOM: She doesn't know a thing.

TOLEN: She knows what she wants, or rather what she will want.

TOM: I don't think you're the right person to give a girl her first experience.

TOLEN: She's an independent human being. Why should you say what's good for her? How old are you, Nancy?

NANCY: Seventeen.

TOLEN: There you are. (*Pause.*) Anyway, she's not really my type. I've had sufficient for today. I'm merely amusing myself. It's more subtle.

TOM: You know what happens to young girls alone in London, don't you?

NANCY: Yes—no—I——

TOM: You'd better find a Catholic Girls' Refuge.

NANCY: I'm not a Catholic.

TOM: You'll find the address in any ladies lavatory in any railway station.

46

NANCY: Oh—I——

TOLEN: How do you know?

NANCY: I think I ought to go—I——

(*Enter* COLIN *with tea things including milk in a bottle.*)

COLIN: That damned stuff in the passage. You'll have to move it.

TOM: I'm not having it in here.

COLIN: I'm not having it in the passage.

TOM: I'm not having it in here.

COLIN: When you take a furnished room, you take the furniture as well.

TOM: Not that furniture.

COLIN: What's wrong with the furniture?

TOM: I'm not having it in here. Put it on the bed. Take it to Copp Street.

COLIN: It's my furniture, you're not selling my furniture.

TOM: You're selling your bed.

COLIN: You're not selling my furniture.

TOM: We'll put it on the top landing.

TOLEN: Outside my room? I think not.

TOM: Inside your room.

COLIN: Oh. Let's have some tea.

(*They start pouring out tea.*)

TOLEN: What's the most frightening building in London?

COLIN: Great Ormond Street Hospital for Children.

(*Pause.*)

TOM: What's that?

COLIN: Great Ormond Street Hospital for Children.

NANCY: That's nice. It's true. That's a nice thing to say.

COLIN: Oh? Do you think so?

(TOLEN *touches* NANCY.)

TOM: Do you know how the elephant got the shape it

47

is? Well, there was once a little piggy animal, see? With two great big front teeth that stuck out. However, there are certain advantages in being big—you know, you can eat off trees and things—like horses——

TOLEN: For you this is remarkably incoherent.

TOM: Thanks. So this animal got big and it grew an enormous great long jaw so it could scoop up the vegetation. An enormous jaw, seven foot long—imagine! As big as a door! Now. A seven-foot jaw involves certain difficulties in getting the food from the front of your jaw to the back . . .

TOLEN: Biscuits?

TOM: It had to use its upper lip to shovel the garbage along.

COLIN: Aren't there some chocolate?

TOM: I ate them. Well, the creature's upper lip began to grow. It grew so big it began to do all the work and the creature didn't bother to use its seven-foot jaw. Now, as you know, any organ not in constant use atrophies so the jaw began to shrivel. (*To* TOLEN) Not that you need . . .

NANCY: Tea?

TOM: *But* the two front teeth——

NANCY: More tea?

TOM: Remained. So you are left with an animal having an extraordinarily long upper jaw and two big front teeth. You're left with an elephant. No problem at all. Yes I would, please.

(TOLEN *touches* NANCY's *arm*.)

NANCY: D'you like it? It's new.

48

TOLEN: You should paint that wall straight away or it'll patch up.

TOM: What?

TOLEN: It will dry blotchy.

TOM: Yes. That's a good idea. Yes!

TOLEN: You wanted to see me?

COLIN: Eh?

TOLEN: That's right.

COLIN: Wanted to see you?

TOLEN: You will.

COLIN: What d'you——

TOLEN: Watch this.

COLIN: What do you mean?

TOM: In cold blood, Colin. In cold blood.

TOLEN: I'll show you how.

TOM: Nancy! (*Angry.*) You should go when you're told.

(TOLEN *takes a copy of* Honey *and lies on the bed.*)

NANCY: Would you like something behind your head?

TOLEN: There is a pillow in the passage.

(NANCY *exits, returns with pillow.*)

TOLEN: Why don't you look at me?

NANCY: I can't.

TOLEN: Why can't you?

NANCY: I'll—I'll——

TOLEN: What?

NANCY: I'll laugh.

TOLEN: Why?

NANCY: You'll make me laugh.

TOLEN: Why?

NANCY: You will.

TOLEN: Will I?

NANCY: Yes.

49

TOLEN: Will I?

NANCY: Yes.

TOLEN: Look at me, laugh! Go on! Look at me, laugh, look at me, go on, look at me, laugh, look at me, look at me.
(*She laughs. She stops laughing. He might kiss her.*)

NANCY: No, no.

COLIN: Ha!

TOLEN: You idiot. Fool.
(*Pause.*)

TOM: Do you like my room?

NANCY: What?

TOM: My room.

NANCY: What! It's not much. There's not much to sit on.

TOM: Sit on the piano.

NANCY: (*irritated*). Aw!

TOM: They clutter up the place so I really must get them on the wall.

NANCY: What?

TOM: The chairs. On the wall.

NANCY: What? Oh, it doesn't matter.

TOM: To get them off the floor. Have I said anything to upset you, Tolen?

TOLEN: Nothing you said could possibly upset me.
(*Pause.*) Why do you try and find rational reasons for your childish impulses?

TOM: Do I disturb you?

TOLEN: You make me smile.

TOM: Ooh! He's annoyed. Oh yes, he's annoyed. Be careful or you might lose control. Ah well. Back to work. Pass me another cup of tea, Nancy.

NANCY: What?

50

TOM: Get me another cup of tea, there's a dear.

NANCY: What do you think I am?

TOM: Oh. (*Pause.*) Sorry.

NANCY: Oh all right. (*She pours out tea for* TOM.)

TOM: Thanks.

NANCY: (*to* TOLEN). Do you want some?

TOLEN: No.

(NANCY *pours out tea for herself. Long pause.*)
All right. She's all yours.

COLIN: Eh?

TOLEN: You have a try.

COLIN: What? Me?

TOLEN: Yes.

(*Long pause.*)

COLIN: Has Cardiff got big docks?

NANCY: What?

COLIN: Has Cardiff got big d-docks?

NANCY: Why ask me?

COLIN: Welsh. I mean—aren't you—don't you come
from Wales?

NANCY: No.

COLIN: It was the name—Jones.

NANCY: Where d'you say the Y.W. was?

COLIN: Oh, it's in Martin's Grove. You have to take a
27 bus, get off at the top of Church Street and
walk down on the left until——

NANCY: It far?

COLIN: Pardon?

NANCY: Is it far?

COLIN: No, not very.

NANCY: Good. I'm going.

COLIN: What?

NANCY: I'm off. I said I'm going. And as for you. As for
you Mr. Mr. Mr. only one name. Mr. no name.

As for you. As for you. As for you . . .
(TOLEN *laughs*.)
That's my *Honey*. Give me my *Honey*.

COLIN: I'll take you. I said I'll take you there.

TOLEN: You want your magazine?
(*She retreats.* TOLEN *follows her. She cannot retreat farther. She slaps him. He kisses her.*)
See? It's not difficult.
(NANCY *bursts into tears*.)

TOM: Well that's that. I need this room, Tolen.

TOLEN: Expecting someone?

TOM: Maybe.

TOLEN: Man or woman? (*Pause*.) Are you a homosexual?

TOM: No. (*Pause*.) Thanks all the same.
(*Exit* TOLEN.)

COLIN: Why do you like annoying him?

TOM: He was annoyed, wasn't he? He's softening up. Ha ha! Now he'll play gramophone records and make telephone calls. Really Colin, what a mess, suppose the Queen were to come. Oh this wall, this sickening, everlasting wall, it's enormous, it goes on for ever. I'm fed up with it. Here.
(*Gives* COLIN *a brush*.)

COLIN: Eh? What's this for?
(TOM *gives* NANCY *a brush*.)

TOM: Only the end bit, the plain bit, the uncreative bit, the bit that don't need genius.

COLIN: You want us to paint the wall?

TOM: The white bit, the boring bit. I'm sick of it.

COLIN: You're so damned lazy.

TOM: Attack it. Attack it.

COLIN: And messy.

NANCY : Yes! Yes! you yes! (*She attacks wall.*) You ha
ha! Yes (*mumbling between her teeth*). Yes!
Um hm um hm!
TOM : A dear girl. A darling girl. There. That's right.
(*Exit* TOM.)
COLIN : Here?
TOM : (*off*). Here?
COLIN : The end.
TOM : (*off*). The window end?
COLIN : Yes.
TOM : (*entering*). That's right.
(*Enter* TOM *with a sheet which he ties round*
NANCY. *She takes her jacket off and gives it to
him.*)
TOM : Ah yes, that's nice. Faster, serfs! (*Pause.*)
Elephants. (*Pause.*) The Indians keep elephants
like we keep cows.—I was wondering how big
an elephant's udder was. My God, imagine it
swishing around. Do you know, in Walt
Disney's early films there were cows and the
censor cut the udders out so he put brassieres
on them, imagine! . . . Jersey cows wear
brassieres, it's true. Jersey cows wear brassieres.
Something wrong here, cows shouldn't need
brassieres. Human beings need them because
they stand upright. They used to go on all fours,
so they hung downwards—vertically—now they
stand upright and it puts on this terrible
strain . . .
(NANCY *is laughing.*)
All right, all right. It's true.
COLIN : Oh——
TOM : Eh?
COLIN : I wish you wouldn't show off.

53

TOM: (*to* NANCY). Hi! (*To* COLIN) I don't show off.

COLIN· You do.

TOM: (*restraining* NANCY). Colin wishes I wouldn't show off.

COLIN: Well you do show off.

TOM: I don't.

COLIN: You do. Stop slapping it.

NANCY: I like slapping.

COLIN: It's splashing.

NANCY: So what?

COLIN: It's dripping.

NANCY: I don't care. I don't care.

COLIN: Don't get so excited.

NANCY: You're talking. I hear you.

COLIN: Look at her. Look at her.

TOM: I see her.

NANCY: So what.

TOM: (*shepherding* NANCY *to a bit of wall away from his careful painting*). Watch it—yes—there's a— and now—that's right—more left.

NANCY: What's the difference between an elephant and a pillar box?

COLIN: They can neither of them ride a bicycle.

NANCY: You knew!

COLIN: What? What?

NANCY: I can reach higher than you.

COLIN: (*holding up his arm*). Heard it before.

NANCY: Yes, I can.

TOM: I don't show off.

COLIN: What? No, you can't.

NANCY: I can.

COLIN: You can't.

TOM: I do——

NANCY: I can——

54

TOM: —sometimes——
NANCY: —look——
COLIN: You don't—I mean——
NANCY: I can reach higher than you——
COLIN: Ouch!
NANCY: What?
COLIN: It's all run up my elbow. Oh.
TOM: You're dripping everywhere. There's a cloth in the kitchen.
(*Exit* COLIN. *Telephone rings* (*off*). *Pause. Enter* TOLEN.)
TOLEN: It's for you.
TOM: Man or woman?
TOLEN: Woman.
(*Exit* TOM. *Pause.* TOLEN *moves to help* NANCY *off with sheet. She avoids him.*)
TOLEN: No one's going to rape you.
NANCY: Oh!
TOLEN: (*laughing*). Girls never get raped unless they want it.
NANCY: Oh!
TOLEN: I'm sorry about—what happened.
NANCY: That's——
TOLEN: It was clumsy—very——
NANCY: That's all right.
TOLEN: It was because they were here—the clumsiness I mean——
NANCY: Was it?
TOLEN: In a way, in a way.
NANCY: Oh.
TOLEN: Don't you believe me?
NANCY: I don't know—I——
TOLEN: Please——
NANCY: I——

TOLEN: Please believe me.

NANCY: It doesn't matter.

TOLEN: It does matter, it matters very much. (*Pause.*) It matters very much to me. (*Pause.*) How sweet you are. Such a sweet face, such sweetness. (*Pause. He kisses her.*) Ssh . . . ssh . . . Come . . . come up . . . come upstairs . . .

NANCY: Oh . . . oh . . .

TOLEN: Come up to my room . . .

NANCY: Oh . . . oh . . . no . . .

TOLEN: You like music? I've got some records upstairs . . . I'll play you some records.
(*Enter* COLIN.)

COLIN: Well, let's get on—oh— . . . Where are you going? Are you going out? To find the Y.W.? I'll come too.

TOLEN: What?

COLIN: I'll come as well.

TOLEN: Where?

COLIN: To find it.

TOLEN: What?

COLIN: The Y.W.
(*Pause.*)

TOLEN: Why don't you go?

COLIN: Eh?

TOLEN: Why don't you go look for the Y.W.?

COLIN: Well, you're coming aren't you?
(TOLEN *is exasperated.*)
Well—you——

NANCY: Oh——

COLIN: Oh come on——

NANCY: I don't think I——

COLIN: Oh please——

NANCY: What about the cases?

56

COLIN: The cases?

NANCY: I can't go without them.

COLIN: He'll look after them.

NANCY: Who will?

COLIN: He will.

TOLEN: Me?

NANCY: Where are you going?

TOLEN: I'm going out.

NANCY: I'd like a walk.

COLIN: So would I.

NANCY: What about the cases?

COLIN: You stay here.

TOLEN: Why should I?

COLIN: You could stay here.

TOLEN: Why should I?

COLIN: You could look after the cases.

TOLEN: He can.

COLIN: Who can?

TOLEN: Tom can.

COLIN: He's upstairs. Can't they stay here?

NANCY: I need them at the Y.W.

(TOLEN *moves away.* NANCY *follows.*)

COLIN: Let's go look for the Y.W.

NANCY: Are you coming?

TOLEN: To the Y.W.?

COLIN: Well, let's you and me go.

NANCY: Well——

COLIN: Well——

NANCY: I don't think I really——

COLIN: You said you did.

NANCY: Did I?

COLIN: Yes.

NANCY: What about the cases?

TOLEN: Why don't you carry them?

COLIN: Me?

TOLEN: If you're going to the Y.W., why don't you carry them?

COLIN: Let's go for a walk.

NANCY: What about the cases?

TOLEN: You carry them.

COLIN: She!

TOLEN: Yes.

COLIN: She can't carry them.

TOLEN: She's already carried them. She carried them here.

COLIN: She can't carry them.

TOLEN: You carry them.

COLIN: I want both hands free.

(*Pause. Enter* TOM. TOLEN *starts to exit.*)

NANCY: Where you going?

TOLEN: Oh, anywhere. D'you want to?

NANCY: D'you want me to?

TOLEN: If you want to.

COLIN: Are you going to the Y.W.?

TOLEN: Maybe.

COLIN: I'll come too.

TOLEN: What about the cases?

(COLIN *picks up the cases.*)

COLIN: I'll come too.

(TOLEN *and* NANCY *exit.*)

TOM: Stay with them, Colin.

COLIN: Eh?

TOM: Stick with them.

(*Exit* COLIN. TOLEN *and* NANCY *are seen to pass window, followed soon after by* COLIN. *Exit* TOM. *Heavy dragging and banging off. Enter* TOM *looking very pleased with himself, takes bed to bits and drags it off. More banging. Enter* TOM

58

*exhausted. Drinks milk. Exits with tray. Re-enters
and resumes painting.* TOLEN *and* NANCY *pass
window. Door is tried (off).* TOLEN *and* NANCY
*enter through window. Both are laughing a good
deal.*)

TOLEN: That door blocked again?

TOM: Been moving a few things.

TOLEN: And if you push it under—ooops! (NANCY
laughs) and over—ooops! (NANCY *laughs.*)
(*Enter* COLIN *through window.*

TOM: You look very seasick.

COLIN: Shut up.

(COLIN *thrusts carrier bag on his head.* NANCY *is
pretty hysterical.* TOLEN *works her up, kissing and
laughing.* TOM *intensifies the atmosphere by
beating a rhythm on bed or step-ladder, possibly
using mouth music as well.*)

TOLEN: We'll go and listen to those gramophone
records.

(*Exit* TOLEN *and* NANCY. TOM *stops beating.
Pause. Large crash (off). Enter* TOLEN.)

TOLEN: Who put that stuff on the stairs?

TOM: Oh, are the stairs blocked?

TOLEN: I can't get up to my room.

TOM: Oh, can't you?

(*Enter* NANCY.)

NANCY: Why's the wardrobe on the stairs—and the
bed—the stairs are blocked . . .

(TOLEN *grabs her.*)

Oh! You're hurting me!

TOM: Stop. Stop that.

NANCY: Let me go! Let me go! Let me go!

(*She escapes but not before* TOLEN *has hurt and
thoroughly frightened her.*)

Don't touch me! (TOM *and* COLIN *attempt to comfort her but they only excite her more*.) Keep off! Keep off! D'you hear? Keep away! Don't touch me! You—you—you—don't touch me! You don't touch me. All right? All right? ... Now, now then, now ... what's—what's up? What is it, eh? Yes? What you—what you want with me?—what you want—What you trying on, eh? What you trying to do? What is it, eh? What you want—you—you—you ... ... Mr. Smart! Mr. Smartie! You think you're— You think you're—You think you're pretty clever. You think you're all right.... You do, don't you, Mr. Smartie! Mr. Tight Trousers! Mr. Tight Trousers! Mr. Narrow Trousers! You think you're the cat's—you think you're ... I'll show you ... I'll show you, Mr. Tight Trousers. Just you don't come near me, d'you hear? Just you don't come near me—come near me, d'you hear? Come near me! I'll show you, Mr. Tight Trousers! Tight Trousers! Yes! Yes! Come near me! Come near me! Come near me! Come! Come! Come! Come! Come!
(TOLEN *laughs and walks away.* NANCY *moans and collapses.* COLIN *somehow catches her as she falls.*)

COLIN: She's fainted!

TOM: Lucky there was someone to catch her.

(*End of Act Two*)

ACT THREE

Before the curtain rises there is a loud banging and crashing, mixed with shouts and cries.
Curtain up.
COLIN *is holding* NANCY *like a sack of potatoes.* TOM *and* TOLEN *are just finishing putting up the bed.*

TOM: Give it a bash! And so—oops! A bedmaker, that's you Tolen, a master bed-wright. O.K. Has she come round yet?

COLIN: Come round?

TOM: Is she still out?

COLIN: Out?

TOM: Oh, he's a thick one. This way.

COLIN: I'm not thick, she's heavy.

TOM: Don't drop her. Now we've got this out of the passage, Tolen, you can go upstairs to bed. We'll put her here to rest. Sling her over. . . . Not like that!

COLIN: You said sling.

TOM: She's in a faint, fainted, can't defend herself.
(*They get* NANCY *on the bed.*)

NANCY: Oh . . . oh dear . . . oh dear . . . I do feel . . . I think I'm going to be——

TOM: Sick?
(NANCY *nods.*)
Not here.

(COLIN *holds out bucket.* TOM *dashes to door and opens it.*)
Bathroom.
(*Exit* NANCY *followed by* TOM. *Pause.* TOLEN *goes to door. Opens it and listens a moment, then closes door and bolts it.*)

COLIN: What are you doing?

TOLEN: I don't want to be interrupted, Colin. I have something I wish to discuss with you.

COLIN: Oh, I see. . . . But this is Tom's room.

TOLEN: This is your room, Colin, your room. You are the landlord. The house belongs to you.
It's for you to say whose room this is, Colin. Who lives here.

COLIN: Oh, yes—er——

TOLEN: There is something I would like to discuss with you, Colin. An idea I had.

COLIN: Oh?

TOLEN: You know that you need help, Colin. You do know that, don't you?

COLIN: Mm.

TOLEN: Now tell me, Colin, how many women have you had?

COLIN: Mm . . .

TOLEN: Two women. Only two. And you were late starting weren't you, Colin? Very late. Not until last year. And Carol left you how many months ago?

COLIN: Mm . . .

TOLEN: Six months ago. That's right, isn't it. Two women in two years. Some of us have more women in two days.

I have a suggestion to make to you, Colin. A
suggestion which you will find very interesting
and which will help you very much. (*Pause.*)
Now as you know, Colin, I have a number of
friends. *Men.* And they can help you Colin, as I
can help you. I am thinking particularly of Rory
McBride.

COLIN: Oh.

TOLEN: Rory McBride is a man, Colin, a clever man,
a gifted man, a man I can respect. He knows a
great many things, Colin. Rory McBride was
doing things at thirteen that you haven't ever
done, Colin; things that you don't even know
about.

COLIN: What sort of things?

TOLEN: In a moment, Colin. First I will tell you my
suggestion. Now, as you know, I have a number of
regular women, Colin. Women I regularly
make. And Rory McBride has a number of
regular women too. Perhaps not quite as many
as I have, but several. Now. Quite
recently, Rory and I were talking—comparing
notes—and we decided it would be a good idea
if we saw each other more often . . . if even we
were to live near each other.

COLIN: Oh?

TOLEN: Yes, Colin . . . perhaps in the same house . . .
and that we would share our women.

COLIN: Oh!

TOLEN: After I have had a woman, Rory can have her,
and if I want I can have Rory's.
Of course Rory realizes that ıt may, in a sense,

63

be dangerous for him. He may lose a few of his
women. However, Rory is well aware that, in
the long run, he will profit by the arrangement;
he will learn much, Colin, from the women who
have been with me.

COLIN: (*agreeing*). Mm.

TOLEN: Now this is the suggestion I have to make. I
would consider allowing you to come in on this
arrangement.

COLIN: Oh!

TOLEN: Yes, Colin.
I would allow you to come in with Rory
and me, share our women. I think you would
learn a great deal, Colin.

COLIN: Oh yes.

TOLEN: It would be a privilege for you, a great privilege.

COLIN: Oh, yes, I see that.

TOLEN: I'm sure Rory will he will agree. (*Pause.*) Now
agree to this, Colin. I will ask him.

COLIN: Do you think he will?

TOLEN: If I ask him, Colin, he will agree. (*Pause.*) Now
what I suggest, Colin, is that Rory moves into
this house.

COLIN: Mm?

TOLEN: In here.

COLIN: Oh . . .

TOLEN: What's the matter, Colin?

COLIN: But there's no room. There's you and me
and——

TOLEN: There is this room, Colin. The room you let to
Tom. (*Pause.*) Remember this is your room.
You are the landlord. Rory could have this

64

room and . . .

(TOM *yells (off) and bangs door.*)

Rory McBride has a Chinese girl, Colin, slinky, very nice, do very well for you.

COLIN: Chinese?

TOLEN: It's only a question of experience. Of course you'll never be quite so——

COLIN: Good as——

TOLEN: Me, but——

COLIN: But still——

TOLEN: Oh yes, I don't doubt——

COLIN: You really think——

TOLEN: Certainly!

COLIN: Chinese!

(*Enter* TOM *through window.*)

TOM: What the hell d'you think you're doing? Why d'you bloody lock the door, Tolen? You bloody remember this is my room.

(*He unbolts door.*)

TOLEN: Oh no, Tom, this is Colin's room.

TOM: Eh? What's going on here?

(*Small crash upstairs.*)

(*Yelling.*) Stop that. What the hell's she up to now? Where's her bag? She wants her bleeding bag. I tell you she's gone bloody funny like a bleeding windmill.

(*Cry off.* TOLEN *crosses the room.*)

TOLEN: Can you not control your women, Tom?

(*Exit* TOM. TOLEN *crosses the room again.*)

TOLEN: And a German girl.

COLIN: German!

(COLIN *crosses the room imitating* TOLEN.)

65

TOLEN : Hold your head up, Colin. Head up! Don't
stick your chin out. Keep your belly in. Bend
your arms slightly at the elbows—not quite so—
that's better. They should swing freely from
your shoulders. . . . Not both together! Keep
your head up! Move! Move! Move! Move! Feel
it coming from your shoulders Colin, from your
chest! From your gut! From your loin! More
loin! More gut, man! Loin! Loin! Move! Move!
Move! Move! Keep your head up! Authority,
Colin! Feel it rippling through you! Authority!
Keep your head up! Authority! Authority!
COLIN : Authority.
TOLEN : Authority! Move! Move! Move! Move!
Authority!
TOM : (*off*). You can have a cup of tea and . . .
NANCY : (*off*). Tea!
TOM : (*off*). Tea.
NANCY : (*off*). I won't touch it.
(*Enter* NANCY *wrapped in a blanket.*)
TOM : (*entering*). For God's sake make her some tea.
NANCY : I won't touch it. What's that?
TOM : What's what?
NANCY : That.
TOM : We've lugged this thing in here so you can lie
down. Now lie down.
NANCY : I never asked you to bring it in.
TOM : You——
NANCY : Don't swear.
(COLIN *walks about the stage.*)
You're not getting me on that thing again I tell
you. Putting that thing together again to tempt
a girl. Hiding it up passages. Stuffing it here and

66

there. What d'you think I am? Eh? Eh? Don't
you hear? Can't you hear what I say?
(NANCY *bares her teeth and growls at* COLIN. *He
is momentarily disconcerted then ignores her and
struts up and down again.*)
An open invitation if you ask me. Ask me! Go
on ask me! Well somebody ask me . . . please
. . . (*Pause.*) A nasty situation. Dear me, yes.
Very nasty, a particularly vicious sense of—
criminal, yes, that's it—positively criminal. They
ought to be told, somebody should—I shall
phone them, phone them—the police, Scotland
Yard, Whitehall one two one two (*she catches
sight of* COLIN *walking up and down*) one two
one two (*she repeats one two one two as often as
necessary*).
(COLIN *picks up the rhythm and they begin to
work each other up.* NANCY *starts to bang the
rhythm.* COLIN *stamps about and slaps himself
until eventually he hurts himself.* NANCY *is
temporarily assuaged.*)

TOM : That's an interesting movement you've got
there, Colin.
COLIN : Oh, d'you think so?
TOM : Very interesting.
COLIN : Tolen taught it me.
TOM : Oh yes?
COLIN : It's got authority.
TOM : Come again?
COLIN : Authority.
TOM : Ah. Let's see it again . . . ah.

(COLIN *demonstrates, then* TOM *has a go.*)

COLIN: You've got to walk from your gut.

TOM: Eh?

COLIN: Your gut.

TOM: Oh I see. I see, I see. Bucket!

COLIN: Eh?

TOM: For a helmet. Bucket! Bucket! Jump to it!
Don't keep me waiting. Bucket!

COLIN: Oh.

(COLIN *jumps for the bucket, offers it to* TOM *who
puts it on* COLIN's *head.*)

TOM: Now I'll show you what authority's really,
Colin. Much more impressive than a carrier—a
helmet. Dominating, brutal.

(TOM *starts banging a 4/4 rhythm and singing the
"Horst Wessel".*)

Ra ra ra ra, ra ra ra ra, march! March! March!
March! Get on with it! Ra ra ra ra.

(NANCY *picks up the 4/4 rhythm and the tune.*)

March! Damn you! March! Jams, guns, guts,
butter! Jams, guns, guts, butter! Boots! Boots!
Boots! Boots! Boots for crushing! Boots for
smashing! Sieg heil! Sieg heil! Ha!

(COLIN *gets rid of the bucket.*)

What's the matter? What's up? Don't you like
it? I thought you loved it. Tolen loves it, don't
you, Tolen? Tolen loves it.

COLIN: Tolen doesn't do that.

TOM: Not so loud maybe, but the same general idea. I
think it's funnier louder, don't you, Tolen?

COLIN: Shut up.

TOM: Just look at Tolen's boots.

(*Pause.* NANCY *jumps up and down.*)

NANCY: Grrr.

TOM: (*disregarding* NANCY *and speaking to* TOLEN).

68

When I die I could be reincarnated as a sea
anemone. It doesn't affect my attitude to death
one little bit but it does affect my attitude to
sea anemones.
A sea anemone with a crew cut would starve to
death. (*Pause.*) Your ears are going red. They're
pulsating red and blue. No, I'm exaggerating.
One is anyway. The one nearest me. (*Pause.*)
That white horse you see in the park could be a
zebra synchronized with the railings.
(TOLEN *moves away.* TOM *looks very pleased.*)

NANCY : I wouldn't touch it if you made it.

TOM : Eh?

NANCY : I wouldn't.

TOM : Made what?

NANCY : Tea.

TOM : (*to* COLIN). You'd better make some.

COLIN : (*disgruntled*). Oh.

TOM : Shall I tell you a story?
(*Exit* COLIN.)
I know you'd like to hear about the kangaroo—
the kangaroo. You heard me. Did you? Now of
course you know that the baby kangaroo lives
in its mother's pouch. Don't you. Go on,
commit yourself.

NANCY : Oh, all right.

TOM : Don't be so cautious. This one is true and pure.
All my stories are true unless I say so. Well, the
baby kangaroo is born about two inches long
and as soon as it's born it climbs into its
mother's pouch—how does it climb? Never
mind, it fights its way through the fur . . .
(COLIN *enters balefully and sets down a tray and
exits.*)

69

When it gets inside the pouch the baby kangaroo
finds one large, solid nipple. Just one. The baby
latches on to this nipple and then it, the nipple,
swells and swells and swells until it's shaped
something like a door knob in the baby's
mouth. And there the baby kangaroo stays for
four months, four solid months. What an
almighty suck! Isn't that interesting? Doesn't it
interest you as a facet of animal behaviour so
affecting human behaviour? Doesn't it make
you marvel at the vast family of which God
made us part? Oh well . . .
(*Pause.*)
NANCY: What happened?
TOM: What happened when?
NANCY: You know when.
TOM: No, I do not.
NANCY: You know when.
(*Enter* COLIN *with teapot.* COLIN *pours out tea in
silence. Hands a cup to* TOLEN, *goes with a cup to*
NANCY.)
What's that?
COLIN: Eh?
TOM: Tea.
NANCY: I'm not having any. I'm not touching it. He's
put something in it.
COLIN: Eh?
TOM: Put something in it?
NANCY: Oh yes, he's put something in it.
TOM: Don't be so daft.
NANCY: I'm not touching it.
TOM: But——
NANCY: I'm not.
TOM: What should he put in it? There's absolutely

70

nothing in it. Nothing at all—look—ugh!—
Sugar!
(*Pause.*)
NANCY: I like sugar.
COLIN: Two.
NANCY: What?
COLIN: Two lumps.
NANCY: I take two.
COLIN: I know.
(*Pause.* NANCY *takes the tea and drinks. Long
pause.*)
NANCY: I've been raped. (*Pause.*) I have.
TOLEN: I beg your pardon.
NANCY: You heard.
COLIN: I didn't.
NANCY: I've been raped.
(TOLEN *sneers audibly.*)
COLIN: What!
NANCY: I have been—it was just after—when I fainted—
there by the—before I went up with—when I
fainted. I was raped.
(TOLEN *sneers.*)
COLIN: When she says——
NANCY: I have been, you did——
COLIN: Does she mean really—I mean, actually?
TOM: What else?
NANCY: Rape. Rape. I—I've been——
COLIN: But——
NANCY: Raped.
COLIN: But you haven't.
NANCY: I have.
COLIN: No one has——
NANCY: Rape.
COLIN: But we've been here all the time, all of us.

71

NANCY: Huh!

COLIN: You know we have.

TOLEN: A vivid imagination, that's what's the matter with her.

NANCY: Eh?

COLIN: Oh?

TOM: Watch it.

TOLEN: Take no notice of her.

NANCY: Eh?

TOLEN: Ignore her.

NANCY: What? Rape?

TOM: You be careful, Tolen.

NANCY: Rape! I been——

TOLEN: She quite simply wishes to draw attention to herself.

NANCY: (*a little unsure*). Oh?

TOLEN: She has fabricated a fantasy that we have raped her. First because she wants us to take notice of her and second because she really would like to be raped.

NANCY: Eh?

COLIN: Would you mind saying that again?

TOLEN: Her saying that we have raped her is a fantasy. She has fabricated this fantasy because she really does want to be raped; she wants to be the centre of attention. The two aims are, in a sense, identical. The fabrication that we have raped her satisfactorily serves both purposes.

COLIN: Oh.

NANCY: What's that word mean? Fabricated?

TOLEN: Made it up.

NANCY: (*a bit nonplussed*). Oh no. Oh no. Not that. I know, oh yes. I'm not having that sort of—I know, oh yes. I'm the one that knows. You've

72

had your fun and—and—there! It was there!
You've had your fun and now I feel funny,
queer, sick. I know, you're not coping with a—
I'm not a fool you know—I'm not a ninny. . . .
No, no, I didn't make it up . . . fabricated . . .
fabricated . . . fabricated . . .

TOM : (*to* TOLEN). What'll you do if she tells everyone
you raped her?

TOLEN : What?

TOM : There's a methodist minister lives two doors
down. Suppose she was to yell out of the
window? By God you'd look silly, you'd look
right foolish. I'd give a lot to see that.

TOLEN : Are you mad?

TOM : (*to* NANCY). Don't let him off so easily love.

NANCY : Eh?

TOM : (*to* TOLEN). What'll you do if she yells down the
street?

NANCY : Rape! They done me! Rape! You done me! You
did! Rape! Rape! Rape! Rape! Rape! (*At
window*) Rape! (*etc. as necessary*).

TOLEN : Shut the window.
(TOLEN *goes for* NANCY.)

NANCY : Rape!
(TOLEN *gets her neatly under control and keeps his
hand over her mouth.*)

TOM : Try and keep your dignity on that one.

COLIN : Mind she doesn't bite.

TOLEN : Shut the window.
(COLIN *shuts the window.* TOLEN *releases* NANCY.)

NANCY : You don't want me yelling down the street, do
you?

TOLEN : We don't want the trivial inconvenience.

73

NANCY : You're scared they'll hear and lock you up.

TOLEN : I do not intend to expose myself to trivial indignities from petty officials.

NANCY : You're worried. You're scared. You're afraid. I'll tell. I will tell!

COLIN : Eh?

NANCY : The police. The Y.W. I'll report you. That's it. The lot. Them all. I'll tell them how you raped me—how you—I'll tell them. The coppers. The Y.W.

TOM : Whew!

NANCY : All the lurid details! All the horrid facts! *News of the World.* TV. Read all about it! Rape! Rape! Just you wait! You'll get ten years for this!

TOM : She means it.

TOLEN : She's simply drawing attention to herself.

COLIN : Means what?

TOM : She means to tell everyone we raped her. Right. (*Putting* TOLEN *on the spot.*) In that case he must rape her.

COLIN : Eh?

TOLEN : I beg your pardon?

TOM : In that case she must be raped by him.

NANCY : I'm not having it twice.

TOM : You want her to keep quiet.

TOLEN : I do not propose to allow her to expose . . .

TOM : (*cutting him short*). Right. You say she's made this up because she really does want to be raped.

COLIN : Well?

TOM : If he wants to keep her quiet he must rape her. According to what he says—and he's probably right—that's the only thing will satisfy her.

74

COLIN: If she's raped she'll be the centre of attention, that's it!

TOM: Just so. What do you say?

(*The men are talking about* NANCY *but, in a sense, have forgotten her. She is resentful.*)

NANCY: Rape!

TOM: What do you say, Tolen?

(*Pause.*)

TOLEN: It's your idea. Why don't you rape her?

TOM: I like her yelling down the street.

(*Pause.*)

TOLEN: Colin?

COLIN: What me? Oh no. I couldn't.

(*Pause.*)

NANCY: Rape!

TOLEN: I never yet came to a woman under duress and certainly never because I was forced to it. Because she demanded it. Because I had to buy her silence. I shall not now.

(NANCY *explodes round the room.*)

NANCY: Ray! Ray! Ray! Ray! Ray! (*continue as long as necessary*).

COLIN: Stop her!

TOLEN: Don't let her——

TOM: Whoops! Whoops!

TOLEN: Near the——

COLIN: What eh?

TOLEN: Shut the door!

COLIN: Ow!

TOLEN: —door!

TOM: Door? Door?

COLIN: Door?

(*A chase. Finally* NANCY *exits down left by mistake.* COLIN *slams door and bolts it.*)

TOLEN: The front. The front door. She'll get out the front. Colin!
(*Exit* COLIN *through window. Banging (off) at front door. Re-enter* COLIN.)
COLIN: No, she won't. It's blocked.
(*Pause.*)
TOM: She smashed up the bathroom. She might——
(*Pause.*)
TOLEN: My records!
(TOLEN *throws himself on the door. Enter* NANCY *barefoot. She wears her pleated skirt thus: her right arm through the placket, the waist band running over her right shoulder and under her left arm. She carries her underclothes, which she scatters gaily.*)
NANCY: Shove you in jug! Put you in jail! One for the road! Long for a stretch! Just you wait! I'll tell!
(*Pause.*)
TOM: That's not how a skirt is usually worn, still it's bigger than a bathing costume.
COLIN: It's not a bathing costume.
NANCY: I shall sue you for paternity.
TOM: Now listen, Nancy.
NANCY: All of you.
TOM: Nancy.
NANCY: Don't Nancy me.
TOM: (NANCY *ad libs through speech*). Look love—don't say anything for a minute. Now look, we haven't raped you—but—just a moment—Now listen, everything's happening so fast you must give us a chance to think. I mean you're a reasonable girl, Nancy, an intelligent girl, give us a chance now, just give us a chance like a reasonable, rational, intelligent girl, just let us

76

talk for one moment. No yelling and no dashing off anywhere.

NANCY: It's a trap.

TOM: No it isn't. I promise. It's pax for one minute.

NANCY: All right. I'll give you one minute.

TOM: That's not enough.

NANCY: Two minutes.

TOM: Five.

NANCY: Three.

TOM: Done.

NANCY: Three minutes and no more. Then I'll start yelling again. Lend me a wrist watch.

TOM: Oh very well. Colin!

NANCY: And if you're naughty and cheat I can smash it.

COLIN: Oh I say——

TOM: Oh come on, Colin.

(COLIN *hands over his watch.* NANCY *climbs step-ladder.*)

Author's Note: the following scene falls into four sections.

1st section: Introduction to the scene: The three confer.)

TOM: Now, Tolen.

TOLEN: The situation is quite clear.

COLIN: Not to me it isn't.

TOM: You've got to rape her.

TOLEN: Please be quiet, Tom.

NANCY: (*while the others confer*).

I've been raped, I've been raped,

I've been raped, raped, raped,

I've been raped, I've been raped, I've been raped.

I've been raped, I've been raped,

77

I've been raped, raped, raped,

I've been raped, I've been raped, I've been raped.

TOM: Oh go on.

TOLEN: An impasse has been reached.

COLIN: She believes we've raped her.

TOM: She's convinced herself.

TOLEN: She's made it up to draw attention to herself and because she wants it.

TOM: She is prepared to report us.

COLIN: Yes, yes.

TOM: Tolen doesn't want that.

COLIN: No, no.

TOM: But he's not prepared to do the other thing.

COLIN: What are we going to do?

(*Pause.*)

TOLEN: She must be examined by a competent physician.

COLIN: What?

TOLEN: A doctor. If she's a virgin——

TOM: Not interfered with——

TOLEN: That lets us out!

COLIN: What if she's not?

(*Pause.*)

TOM: If she's not a virgin she could say we raped her and we'd have a job to prove otherwise.

TOLEN: She must be a virgin.

TOM: Why should she be?

TOLEN: Well, take a look at her.

NANCY: Two minutes gone. One minute to go.

TOLEN: Obviously a virgin.

TOM: I don't see why, it doesn't necessarily follow.

COLIN: Follow what?

NANCY: Finished?

TOM: No.

NANCY: Ninety seconds to go.

78

COLIN: Mind the watch.

NANCY: Rape!

TOLEN: Don't get so excited, Colin.

COLIN: It's my watch.

> 2nd section: TOM begins to enjoy the humour of the situation, and states his attitude; so that TOLEN also states *his* attitude.

TOM: Since you take this attitude, there seems no rational course other than to negotiate. Open negotiation.

TOLEN: Negotiate!

TOM: Negotiate.

TOLEN: Negotiate with a woman. Never.

TOM: Then what is your suggestion?

TOLEN: Authority.

COLIN: Oh?

TOLEN: Authority.

COLIN: Ah!

TOLEN: In all his dealings with women a man must act with promptness and authority—even, if need be, force.

COLIN: Force?

TOM: Force?

TOLEN: Force.

> 3rd section: COLIN decides that TOLEN's attitude is correct.

TOM: I cannot agree to force and certainly not to brutality.

TOLEN: Never negotiate.

TOM: Calm, calmth.

NANCY: Sixty seconds.

TOLEN: Force.

79

TOM : Negotiate. Parley, parley.

TOLEN : Negotiate with a woman——

TOM : Calm.

TOLEN : Never! Force!

COLIN : He's——

TOLEN : Force. Force.

COLIN : For——

TOM : Calm, calm, calmth.

TOLEN : Force, force. Never negotiate.

COLIN : For—for——

TOM : No brutality!

COLIN : Force!

TOLEN : Never negotiate! Eh?

COLIN : Force! Force!

TOM : Oh!

COLIN : Force! Force! In dealing with a w-w-w-w—

NANCY : Forty seconds to go!

COLIN : —w-woman a man must act with promptness and authority.

TOLEN : Force.

COLIN : Force.

4th section: COLIN is precipitated into a forceful course of action.

TOM : Parley, negotiate.

TOLEN : Authority.

TOM : Parley.

TOLEN : Force.

COLIN : Force.

TOM : No, no, parley, parley!

COLIN : Force.

TOLEN : Force.

NANCY : Twenty.

TOM : Parley, parley.

80

TOLEN: No, no. Force.

COLIN: For! For! For! He's right!

NANCY: Ten seconds to go.

COLIN: Force.

(*The following should tumble across each other as the excitement mounts.*)

TOLEN: Force.

TOM: Parley.

NANCY: Eight.

COLIN: Force.

TOLEN: Never negotiate.

TOM: Calm.

COLIN: He's right, he's absolutely——

TOLEN: Force.

NANCY: Four.

COLIN: A man——

NANCY: Three.

COLIN: Must——

NANCY: Two.

COLIN: Use——

NANCY: One.

COLIN: Force. (*Slight pause.*) Shut up! Just you shut your—d'you hear! You're talking through you—Firmness! A firm hand! Spanking! See who's—I've been here all the time, d'you hear? All the time. You've not been raped. You have not. I know. So stop squawking. I know. I've been here all the time.

NANCY: Ah.

COLIN: I've been here all the time. So I can prove, prove, testify. I have seen nothing. You've not been raped. I know. I've been here all the time.

NANCY: Ah.

COLIN: Come on down now and get them on. Get your

81

clothes on. Come down, come down you silly
little . . . little messer. You've not been raped, I
know. I've been here all the time.

NANCY: You!

COLIN: I've been here all the time!

NANCY: You did it! It was you!

COLIN: I been here . . . eh?

NANCY: You! You! You! You! He's it! He did it! He
raped me! He's been here all the time! He says
so! He has! He did it! Yes, he raped me!

COLIN: Me!

NANCY: You.

TOM: Him!

COLIN: Me!

NANCY: Yes, you. You been here all the time.

TOM: You, she says. She says you did it.

COLIN: Me.

NANCY: Yes. You'll get ten years.

COLIN: Me, me? Me! Oh no. This is awful.
You're making a terrible mistake.

NANCY: Oh no, not likely.

COLIN: Oh, oh you are—tell her someone. Someone,
Tolen, tell—her I didn't. No really, I mean——

NANCY: I got a head on my shoulders.

COLIN: I can see that but——

NANCY: That's it, you. You raped me.

COLIN: But—but I assure you—I mean——

NANCY: That's him, officer, that's the one.

COLIN: No! Tolen—Tom—please. I mean I didn't
really I didn't.

NANCY: Clothes!

COLIN: Clothes?

82

NANCY: Tore them off me.

COLIN: Tore the—oh no.

NANCY: Scattered.

COLIN: No.

NANCY: There they are.

TOM: Clear evidence.

NANCY: That face. You'd never know, they'd never guess.

COLIN: Oh, wouldn't they?

NANCY: No girl would ever suspect.

COLIN: Oh?

NANCY: But underneath——

COLIN: What?

NANCY: Raving with lust.

COLIN: Oh no, I mean——

NANCY: Fangs dripping with blood.

COLIN: Oh.

NANCY: Bones of countless victims hidden in the basement.

COLIN: We haven't got a basement. No! No! I mean I didn't, really I didn't. I didn't rape you—I mean I wouldn't—but well—this is terrible! Me! . . . You really think I did?

NANCY: Of course.

COLIN: I mean you really do think I did?

NANCY: Yes.

COLIN: You really do!

NANCY: Wait till next Sunday. What's your job?

COLIN: Eh? Im a teacher.

NANCY: Schoolteacher rapes—rapes—rapes—Nancy Jones!

COLIN: Oh!

83

NANCY: Little did the pupils at—at——
COLIN: Tottenham Secondary Modern——
NANCY: Tottenham Secondary Modern realize that beneath the handsome exterior of their tall, fair-haired, blue-eyed schoolteacher there lurked the heart of a beast, lusting for the blood of innocent virgins—little did they—You wait till you see the *Sunday Pictorial*.
COLIN: Oh, I say, me. Me. Me. Oh I say. Oh. Oh. Do you really think——?
NANCY: What?
COLIN: I've got a handsome exterior?
NANCY: Well—rugged perhaps, rather than handsome. And strong.
COLIN: Oh.
NANCY: Oh yes, ever so. And lovely hands.
COLIN: Oh. Oh. Oh. . . . Are you—are you doing anything tonight?
NANCY: What?
COLIN: Are you doing anything tonight?
NANCY: Oh!
COLIN: Oh, please, I didn't mean that. I mean I didn't rape you, anyway, I mean, oh well. Look, I mean let's go to the pictures or something or a walk or a drink or anything please. I think you're simply—I mean—Oh golly—do you really think I did? I mean I didn't rape you but I would like to—I mean, I would like to take you to the pictures or something.
NANCY: Well, I don't know it doesn't seem quite—I mean after——

COLIN: Oh please——
NANCY: Well——
COLIN: The pictures or anything.
NANCY: Would you?
COLIN: Oh, yes, I would.
TOLEN: This I find all very amusing.
TOM: I thought you might.
TOLEN: Hilarious.
TOM: I've always admired your sense of humour.
COLIN: Eh?
TOM: Well done. Very good. You're getting on very nicely, Colin. Much better than the great Tolen.
TOLEN: That sexual incompetent.
COLIN: Eh?
NANCY: He's not incompetent. What's incompetent?
TOM: No good.
NANCY: No good? He's marvellous, he raped me.
TOLEN: You have not been raped.
NANCY: I have.
TOLEN: You have not been raped and you know it.
NANCY: He raped me.
TOLEN: You have not.
NANCY: I have.
TOLEN: And certainly not by——
NANCY: Rape.
TOLEN: Him. He wouldn't know one end of a woman from the other.
NANCY: Rape, rape.
TOLEN: The number of times I've seen him. "Has Cardiff got big docks?" He'll never make it never.
COLIN: What?

85

TOLEN: Granted——
COLIN: What did you say?
NANCY: He raped me.
TOLEN: Granted he might do better with help—and he needs help. Bow-legged, spavin-jointed, broken-winded, down and out. Look at him.
COLIN: Eh?
NANCY: He's rugged.
TOLEN: I ask you is it possible——?
NANCY: Handsome.
TOLEN: Or likely——?
NANCY: Marvellous, super.
TOLEN: It takes him four months hard labour to get a girl to bed.
NANCY: He did, you did, didn't you?
TOLEN: That oaf.
NANCY: Go on, tell him.
COLIN: Hard labour?
TOLEN: You keep out of this.
NANCY: Yes, you shut up.
TOLEN: A rapist, oh really.
NANCY: Rape. Rape.
TOLEN: That chicken.
NANCY: Rape.
TOLEN: How stupid can you get? Too ridiculous.
NANCY: Rape. Rape.
TOLEN: Probably impotent.
(TOM *begins to knock a nail into the wall about nine feet above floor level. His banging deliberately punctuates the following.*)
COLIN: Why not?
TOLEN: What?
COLIN: Why not me, pray?
NANCY: Rape. Rape.

COLIN : Why not me? (*To* TOM) Be quiet. (*To* TOLEN)
Sexually incompetent! Hard labour!
(NANCY *starts to chirrup round the room,* COLIN
while talking at the others follows after her.)
NANCY : Rape pape pape pape pape pape——
(TOM *is banging.*)
COLIN : (*to* TOM). Shut up. (*To* TOLEN) Now you
listen——
TOM : Rape!
NANCY : R e e e e e e ep.
COLIN : All, all I can say is out—out—outrage. Outrage.
Outrage. (*To* TOM) Shut up. (*To* TOLEN) Rape,
rape, didn't I? Couldn't I? I did—I mean I
could—(*to* TOM) Shut up. (*To* TOLEN) Now you
listen, now get this straight—(*to* TOM) Shut up.
(*To* TOLEN) I am not incapable!
NANCY : Pay pay pay pay pay pay pee pee pee pee pee
pee.
COLIN : (*to* NANCY). Really, I didn't, really, I wouldn't
mind—(*to* TOM) Shut up, be quiet. (*To* NANCY)
I'd love to—I mean. (*To* TOM) Shut up!
(NANCY *is now keeping up an almost permanent
yelp.* TOM *starts on another nail in another wall.*)
Shut up, shut up. Now get this, get this—get—
get—shut up—I could've yes. I could've if I'd
wanted—rape her—shut up—I didn't—you
think I couldn't—shut up—I—I—Shut! Shut!
I'll show you!
(COLIN *starts to chase* NANCY *round the room.*
TOM'*s banging covers the chase and stops at the
end of it.*)
Just let me—get her—I'll—I'll show you—I'll—
I'll—yes I'll—just you I'll show—oh—oh—oh—
oh—oh——

NANCY: Oh—oh—oh—oh——
(*A chase with objects.*)
COLIN: Oh—oh—oh—oh——
NANCY: Oh—oh—oh—oh——
TOLEN: You can't even catch her Colin, can you? Never
mind rape her. I think you are quite incapable
of making a woman, Colin. Look, I'll show you.
COLIN: If you touch her—
—I'll kill you!
(*Very long pause.* TOLEN *releases* NANCY *who
goes to* COLIN. *A girl passes the window.* TOLEN
laughs gently and then exits through window.
TOM *hoists chair on to the nails in the wall.*)
TOM: Ah yes, beautiful.
(TOM *hoists second chair on to nails.*)
Ah, yes.
(*Exit* TOM.)

(*The End*)

THE SPORT
OF MY MAD MOTHER

A Play

'All creation is the sport
of my mad mother Kali'

HINDU HYMN

PREFACE TO THE NEW VERSION

The Sport of My Mad Mother was not written intellectually according to a prearranged plan. It was shaped bit by bit until the bits felt right in relation to each other and to the whole. It is an anti-intellect play not only because it is about irrational forces and urges but because one hopes it will reach the audience directly through rhythm, noise and music and their reaction to basic stimuli.

The play is written to be acted: nothing is put into words that cannot be shown in action. Very often the words counterpoint the action or intensify the action by conflicting with it. Most of the people in the play distrust emotion and haven't the means to express it anyway and they tend to say things which they think will sound good. But at the same time they betray their real feeling either by what they do, or by the very fact that they need to assume a mask.

It has taken me some years to understand that the play is based upon myth and uses ritual. Myth is the bodying forth in images and stories of our deepest fears and conflicts. *The Sport of My Mad Mother* is concerned with fear and rage at being rejected from the womb or tribe. It uses a very old myth in which a man, rejected by his mother, castrates himself with a stone knife.

We create rituals when we want to strengthen, celebrate or define our common life and common values, or when we want to give ourselves confidence to undertake a com-

5

mon course of action. A ritual generally takes the form of repeating a pattern of words and gestures which tend to excite us above a normal state of mind; at the climax of the rite the essential nature of something is changed (e.g. the mass, a marriage service, the bestowal of diplomas, etc.). This play proceeds by rituals because the insecure and inarticulate group of people who figure in the play depend on them so much.

I have always been dissatisfied with the last act. The play was originally written to a deadline, and had I had more time I think I would have discovered then the principle upon which I have now made the alterations. What has changed in the new version? CALDARO has become DEAN, CALDARO was originally conceived as a swashbuckling Neapolitan/American, he gradually changed as it became clear that GRETA needed a tighter, more conventional liberal/intellectual to oppose her. I used to think that the play was about the conflict between GRETA and CALDARO, and while this remains superficially true I find that, at a much deeper level, it is about the relationship between GRETA and CONE. The character of STEVE (FLIM in the earlier version) was originally slightly unpleasant, but STEVE should be the link between GRETA and the audience and the means whereby she may, perhaps, be controlled.

ANN JELLICOE

February 1964

6

PRODUCTION NOTES

The stage comes forward to meet the audience and there is no precise architectural detail to mark where the stage ends and the auditorium begins.

STEVE sits downstage with several instruments and makes sounds (not necessarily music) rough or sweet, discordant or harmonious, rhythmical or arhythmic. These heighten scenes of excitement and may also give the cue to action.

The verses or poems etc., should be chanted or distorted according to the needs of character and situation. They may be pointed or emphasized by STEVE.

True blue. In Act 2 PATTY refers to the colour true blue. When this scene was first written *Vogue* magazine had named "true blue" as the colour of the season. Where possible and suitable substitute the current seasonal colour to which *Vogue* has given its blessing.

CAST

STEVE

Dean, a young American

PATTY, 17 years old

FAK, about 18 years old

CONE, about 19 years old

DODO, maybe a girl about 13 years old, maybe
an old woman

GRETA, an Australian

9

The Sport of My Mad Mother was originally produced at the Royal Court theatre on 25th February 1958 with the following cast:

FLIM (Steve)	Anthony Valentine
CALDARO (Dean)	Jerry Stovin
PATTY	Sheila Ballantine
FAK	Philip Locke
CONE	Paul Bailey
DODO	Avril Elgar
GRETA	Wendy Craig

Directed by George Devine and Ann Jellicoe
Designed by Jocelyn Herbert

ACT ONE

Down behind a back street, a protected corner.

Enter STEVE, *a young man fairly tall and well built.
Pleasantly and informally dressed with care and taste so that
he is "with it" rather than "way out".* STEVE *doesn't fuss, he
lets events flow round him, but there is something decisive
about his manner and he looks as if he wouldn't let people
push him around much.*

STEVE *brings onstage a drum, motor horn, triangle, cym-
bals, etc., which he arranges on one side of the stage. He
speaks as he works.*

STEVE: (*striking the triangle*). Pure and clear, very low
　　　harmonic content—practically a pure tone.
　　　(*Possibly trying another instrument.*) I like playing
　　　percussion, it's not difficult and it's satisfying—
　　　(*a little amused at himself*)—releases frustrations.
　　　I don't do it professionally, this job's just part
　　　time. I'm not a musician but I do effects here
　　　for the—(*gesturing to acting area*). I'm here—
　　　to—well to have a look—I like seeing how
　　　things work, what life's got to offer, I wanted
　　　to see what there was to theatres and acting.
　　　(*Possibly playing as he talks.*) Everyone's vaguely
　　　interested in the theatre, not many people know
　　　as much as they think they do. I was in an
　　　electronics firm after I left training college—

11

made valves and cathode ray tubes.
They had a special training course so I know
quite a lot about electronics. Now I'm with an
accountant—I like figures—They send me out
to the different firms and I go through the
books and draw up preliminary statements. You
get to know how a business really works when
you go through the books; the figures mean
something, they have something real behind
them. That's what interests me about theatre:
it's not real. I mean a play is just something
that somebody has made up. And yet—I don't
know—it's curious—anyway that's why I'm
here, it interests me, I can sit here and watch
and play. (*Possibly playing.*) I enjoy playing, oh
yes, it's my way of relaxing, I like instruments,
the way they're made and the sounds they
make. But what I like most is the way music
reaches into you. I just want to reach people I
want to make them feel, and with music
somehow . . . music communicates, it reaches
into people and they can forget their brains,
their intellects and the way they've been taught
to intellectualize about everything, they can
just let music happen, let it happen physically
to them. (*He plays a little.*) Mmm. . . .
(*Enter* DEAN, *a young American dressed with a
little more formality than* STEVE *but with an air
of expensive relaxation, possibly he wears
dark-rimmed spectacles. A good-looking,
intelligent and sensitive man.*)

DEAN: As you go down the main road there's a side
street running off—you see them all over
London—the houses are small, two or three

12

storeys high with dirty bits of net curtain in the windows . . . why dirty? . . . Why don't they wash them? . . . Who's "they"? . . . There's a little newsagent on one corner and an empty shop boarded up on another—why empty? Why boarded up? As you pass you can feel a kind of dampness. There's an old woman looking at you from behind some of those net curtains: you can feel her eyes following you as you walk on—not quite stabbing you in the back but kind of daring you. Half-way down the street there's an alleyway: there's ashcans at the entrance and at the bottom the alley seems to turn . . . why not old woman?—It's a free country! You walk down the alley and you wonder what goes on round the corner. . . .
(*Enter* PATTY, *17 years old, a pretty little cockney girl with a lot of make-up round her eyes. She is looking at a home permanent wave outfit. Enter* FAK, *about 18 years old, built loose and big, dressed in real flash clothes. He carries a box which he sets down. Enter* CONE, *a little older than the other two, careless of his clothes, but they are essentially sharp and he looks thin, small and tough.*)

PATTY : (*to the audience*). Have a good look. You'll know me next time.

FAK : (*bringing out a gun which he points at* STEVE). Bang! Bang! Bet that give you a turn.

STEVE : They got me.

PATTY : You look after your drum.

CONE : (*stopping the others with a gesture*). Hey! (*He listens.*)

FAK : Hear anything?

13

CONE: Thought I . . . (*Signalling* FAK *to carry on.*) No.

FAK: Wotcher! Bang bang! Fireworks. Ten bob a box.

CONE: Genuine atomic dynamite.

FAK: Cor what a blast. Bang bang.

CONE: Hydrogen! Plutonium! Uranium! You won't get them in no emporium.

PATTY: ⎫
         (*counting curlers in her home perm outfit*). One, two, three, four, five, six . . . six small ones. One, two, three, four, five, six, seven, eight, nine, ten, eleven, twelve. . . . Mind you don't hurt yourselves.

FAK: ⎬ (*together*) ⎨ (*to audience*) Surprise packet.

CONE: Mystery bunch of big trouble.

FAK: Six bob a box.

CONE: Five bob.

FAK: Four bob.

CONE: ⎭ No fooling, no kidding. Look what you're getting for your money. (FAK *and* CONE *open the box.*)

FAK: Aw shut up.

PATTY: Thirteen, fourteen, fifteen . . .

CONE: What!

FAK: No!

CONE: Unrepeatable!

FAK: Unbelievable!

CONE: Stick it up a car exhaust.

FAK: Rip off the silencer.

CONE: Burst a tyre if you're lucky.

FAK: Two and a tanner at Woolie's.

CONE: Atomic cannon! . . . And six king-size Chinese crackers—real fire—plenty big bang!

14

FAK: Just the job for a bow wow's wagger. Wham! Whack! Clack! Splam!

CONE: Packet of sparklers: let the kiddies blind each other! Did I say four shillings? I don't ask four bob——

FAK: I don't ask three and a kick——

CONE: I don't ask three shillings——

FAK: Two and a tanner!

CONE: Half a dollar! Reach the moon on a Jet Morgan sky rocket.

PATTY: There should be another big one, have I been done?

CONE: Hey! (*He listens, motions* FAK *to look outside,* FAK *does so.*)

FAK: No.

PATTY: Are you listening for something?

CONE: Please to remember the fifth of November. (CONE *sees something inside the box.*) Whow!

PATTY: Instructions read carefully.

CONE: (*throwing the firework to* FAK). Lamp that.

PATTY: Firmly wind strand to root of hair . . .

FAK: There's gunpowder here.

PATTY: Thoroughly moisten with cotton wool dipped in wave lotion . . .

FAK: This'll give us a giggle.

PATTY: It must be strong, it don't half pong.

FAK: And uncle was going to raffle it. . . . Here, catch!

CONE: Catch!

FAK: Catch!

PATTY: Do you mind, I'm trying to read.

CONE: She's reading! Ah hah! What you doing, Patty?

FAK: What you doing, Patty?

15

CONE: What you doing, Patty?

PATTY: Aw shut up.

CONE: She's reading.

FAK: What'll Greta say to this, eh? What'll she say to this?

PATTY: (*irritated*). Aw Greta!

FAK: (*teasing her*). Aw Greta! Greta! Greta!

PATTY: Aw Greta! Greta! Greta! Greta!
(CONE *laughs and goes and looks outside.*)

PATTY: What you got there? . . . Well?

FAK: Something'll take the curl out of your hair.

PATTY: Where'd you nick it?

FAK: Hah hah.

PATTY: Bet there wasn't a copper for miles.

FAK: Couldn't bloody matter.

PATTY: Blow up Buckingham Palace! Oh no. Might upset Greta.

FAK: Aw shut up.

PATTY: Bet you bought it.

FAK: What?

PATTY: Bought it I betcher.

FAK: Wet, she says we're wet.

CONE: Nothing doing, Patty?

FAK: Slack Alice?

PATTY: Look to yourself, Faky-boy.

CONE: Look to yourself, Faky-boy.

FAK: Look to yourself, Faky-boy.

CONE: Seen you somewhere.

FAK: Somewhere before.

PATTY: Big act.

CONE: Sweetie peetie Patty-paws. Beat! Beat!

FAK: Going my way?

PATTY: Catch me——

CONE: Catch me.

16

FAK: Catch me.

CONE: Catch me, Patty-paws, who'd ever have thought?

PATTY: Oh, give over.

CONE: Give over.

FAK: Give over.

PATTY: Give over. Give over.

CONE: Give over, sweetheart.

FAK: Lovey dovey, night night.

PATTY: Leave me be, I never!

CONE: She never.

FAK: She never ever.

CONE: She never ever what?

FAK: What did she never ever?

CONE: She never ever been with nobody—what, nobody? No! No! No! Nobody.

PATTY: Stop it! Stop it!

CONE & If you see a big fat woman.

FAK: Standing on a corner humming.
That's fat Jessie.

PATTY: Is that so.

CONE & If you see her in the pictures

FAK: With a bag of dolly mixtures
That's fat Jessie.

PATTY: Is that so.

CONE & If you see her in a shop.

FAK: Sobbing on a great big mop.
That's fat Jessie.

FAK: (*bringing out his gun*). Yah!
(PATTY *screams*.)

FAK: Always scares birds.

CONE: Shut up. (*Listening*.)

PATTY: What?

CONE: Be quiet.

PATTY: You expecting someone? . . . Who? . . . Who!
Who!

CONE: Shut up. . . . Where d'you nobble it?

FAK: My Dad. He knocked it off a Jerry depot in
the war. Got a lovely axe but he had to chuck
it away. Plenty of ammo too.

PATTY: You want to be careful.

FAK: Kill a feller easy.

PATTY: Put it away, you soppy thing. You're talking
silly.

FAK: Don't you lip me! Don't you lip me like that!

PATTY: You'll get hung.

FAK: That's for stupid fellers. That's for stupid
fellers.

CONE: Relax. . . . Hands is quieter . . . see . . . there's
a spot there—just there (CONE *demonstrates on
the base of* FAK'*s skull*) and you hit—so.

FAK: Here go easy. . . . There?

CONE: Just there.

FAK: There.

CONE: Stick to the gum, chum. This requires finesse.
. . . Better keep it from—she don't like raw
gats.

FAK: (*uncertain*). Oh, I dunno, I dunno.
(PATTY *laughs and taking some nail varnish from
her handbag starts to paint her nails.*)

PATTY: Was I with you lot Friday week?

FAK: Went to the flicks.

PATTY: Friday before that.

CONE: Went to the dogs.

FAK: That's right. There was a shell-out and us and
some of the fellers went to the dogs.

PATTY: Ah . . . that's when Maureen did my hair.

CONE: How d'you keep your nails so long?

18

FAK: She never washes up.

PATTY: Don't be daft.

FAK: Nice smell.

CONE: Give me that. I'll do it a sight better than you.
(*To* FAK *indicating the exit*) Keep yourself
awake.
(CONE *paints* PATTY's *nails.*)

CONE: (*whistling through his teeth*).
Bang bang bang and bish bish bish
Bang bang bang and cosh cosh cosh
Aldgate pump it ain't what it used to be
Poor old Aldgate pump. O!

PATTY: I never seen that blond feller since.

FAK: What feller?

PATTY: Since we went to the pictures with him—you
know, the tall feller, blond and quite good
looking really. . . . What happened to him?

CONE: What happened to who?

PATTY: The feller I was sitting by . . . what was his
name?

CONE: Didn't go with no one else.

PATTY: Are you potty? He sat between me and you:
Fak then me then him then—Garry—Garry,
um, Garry . . .

CONE: (*jabbing her hand*). Shut up.

PATTY: Oo! Mind my nails. That hurt. . . . My Ma'd
slay me if she caught me with this on!

FAK: Go on, bet you beat her.

PATTY: Could be.

FAK: What's stopping you going off on your own?

PATTY: Oh . . .

FAK: Scared?

PATTY: What me?—I wouldn't like to live on my own,
that's all.

19

FAK: Why live on your own?

PATTY: Eh?

CONE: Are you not the flipping virgin.

PATTY: You keep your gob straight. . . . I couldn't, I
can't, . . . I'll not be another Connie.

CONE: Eh? . . . Did you leak?

FAK: Yes, I told her and I told her to keep her
mouth shut.

PATTY: I haven't told anybody.

CONE: Get this: It won't be me that'll be at you if
you do.

PATTY: I've said I haven't told anybody, haven't I?

FAK: And don't you neither.

PATTY: I haven't.

CONE: Keep still . . . just remember: it won't be me.

PATTY: . . . Any day, any time of day, any night . . . in
the streets, or the flicks or an espresso . . .
(CONE *laughs gently*.)

FAK: Bet I can hit that harder than you. Bet I can
hit it so it falls down.

PATTY: You'll break your fist.

FAK: Bet I can hit so——

CONE: Quiet!

PATTY: What you listening for?

CONE: Shut up! (*Listening*.)

PATTY: What! What's happened? Has something
happened?

CONE: Aw sit down and keep still. I haven't finished
yet.

PATTY: Well has it?

CONE: Has what?

PATTY: I don't know.

CONE: Well, what you flapping about?

FAK: (*hitting the wall*). They're yeller! They're yeller!

20

Ha ha! Bang! Bang! Bang! Bang!

PATTY : Aw shut up.

FAK : Bang! Bang!

CONE : You keep over there. (*Indicating the exit.*)

FAK : Why don't you take a turn?

CONE : I'm busy.

PATTY : Tell us about her and Ronny.

FAK : I told you that.

PATTY : Tell me again.

CONE : For crying out loud.

FAK : She had it in for Ronny so he hid himself and she let him. But she knew where he was and he knew she knew.

CONE : (*lyrical sarcastic*). And she knew he knew she knew.

FAK : And he knew if he stepped out he'd get trod on.

PATTY : And he had to, didn't he? He just had to. He got all sort of excited and dreamy of the thought of it and he couldn't stop himself. He had to—come out. . . . And she saw to it. She fixed it. I bet it give you kicks. I bet he had kicks in there just waiting and dreaming. I bet he got all worked up.

(CONE *laughs quietly.*)

I wish I was—I wish I was Greta. Greta! . . . Like spit on a hot plate that's her. Razzle dazzle. It's like—it's like she hits 'em and heps 'em. Anyone'll do anything for her. She'll have Solly caper down Blackpool pier with no clothes on and bash a copper with a Pepsi-Cola bottle. It's like she makes something come busting out. Everyone's got something inside and she makes it grow and grow and come

21

busting out. She looks at Solly. Solly fights
Bobby and first thing they know they're down
the end of the street fighting anyone they see.
And she picks them up and chucks them round
her head and that four is fighting eight and the
eight's fighting sixteen: the whole street's
fighting. It'll start with one fight and then the
whole street—all exploding and growing and
exploding, and every bit of every explosion
makes everything round it explode. The whole
street's fighting—the whole block—the whole
country—the sea—the air—all the planets. And
she stands there, her eyes glittering and
sparkling and laughing the whole time. Bearing
it. Bearing it.

CONE: (*painting his finger-nail*). Cute ain't it.

PATTY: O! Let's go somewhere. Get something started.
. . . It's Guy Fawkes. It's Guy Fawkes. . . . I
never been on a bash. I want—I want to know!
It's Guy Fawkes. . . . You'd do it for her. . . .
(FAK *and* CONE *exchange glances.*)
Is it . . . is it . . . her . . . eh?

FAK: Sort of.

PATTY: Ha ha her! Her!

FAK: Aw shut up.

PATTY: Ha ha! A game eh? What a joke. Oh men! Oh
men like being fooled. You men! You men!
Men! Ha ha! You men are in for a joke you
are! A surprise! A surprise!

FAK: Eh?

PATTY: Tell me, Faky—why you like eh?

CONE: Who says he likes her?

PATTY: She sends you doesn't she? She really sends
you.

22

FAK: Aw shut up.

PATTY: You'd do anything for her—anything.

FAK: Shut up! Shut up!

CONE: Hark, louse. I love you.

FAK: Shut up!

PATTY: Shut up shut up says Faky-white-with-fear.

FAK: I'm not afraid of her.

CONE: You're jealous.

PATTY: Jealous! Jealous! Me! You're all—no minds of your own. Men! My stars! Jealous! And she's not even clean. Men! And she has the lot of you—the lot—Harrow Road—the lot! And all for someone who's—for a woman who's——

CONE: Sweet feminine bitch.

PATTY: You said . . . you said . . . you said—she's not nice.

FAK: What!

PATTY: You did.

FAK: I didn't.

CONE: She ain't nice.

FAK: She is.

PATTY: She isn't.

FAK: She is.

PATTY: You say she isn't.

CONE: Spare me.

PATTY: And I don't understand you and I never will. You. You and all the others! All the others! What about them?

FAK: What?

PATTY: What about them. What about them.

CONE: What about them?

PATTY: The gang. The gang.

CONE: (*mocking*). The gang! The gang!

PATTY: The gang! The gang! The gang she runs! She

23

runs the protection! Pay up or squeeze! Break
your windows break your bones! Pay up or
scream!

CONE: Shut up.

PATTY: Aw! Greta'll hear! Greta! Greta! Greta! And
the joke—the joke! Ha ha! Hop! Hop! But
you'll soon see! You'll see! . . .

CONE: Quiet. Listen. (*Trying to hear something
outside.*)

PATTY: Changing isn't she? Changing!

CONE: (*to* FAK). Stop her. Clout her.

PATTY: Listening for Greta? Looking for Greta, eh?
Why's she not here, eh? Changed! She's
different! And it's going to get worse. Worse.
Bah! Mummy's boy Master Coney! Doesn't
love him any more! She! She! She's losing
interest and especially in Master Coney!
(CONE *turns on her.*)
. . . I . . . I . . .

FAK: (*inarticulate, trying to distract* CONE). Ah.

CONE: Eh?

FAK: . . . Dolly.

CONE: Dolly?

FAK: Dolly!

CONE: *Dolly?*

FAK: Dolly.
(CONE *turns to* PATTY *again.* FAK *goes to her
other side and by his desperation draws* CONE's
attention beyond her.)
Dolly! Dolly!

CONE: Dolly?

FAK: Dolly!

CONE: Dolly!

FAK: Dolly.

24

CONE: Dolly.

FAK: Dolly.

(CONE *and* FAK *have hypnotized each other.*
PATTY *tries to get away and in so doing draws
them on to her.*)

FAK: (*at* PATTY). Dolly.

CONE: (*at* PATTY). Dolly.

FAK: Dolly.

CONE: Dolly.

FAK: Dolly.

PATTY: Shoo.

FAK: Shoo.

PATTY: Shoo.

CONE: Shoo.

FAK: Shoo. Shoo.

PATTY: Shoo. Shoo.

CONE: Shoo. Shoo.

(PATTY *screams.*)

PATTY: (*to audience as if drowning*). Help! Help me!
Help!

DEAN: Stop . . . (*He walks into their midst.*) . . . What
goes on here?

PATTY: Eh?

FAK: Them. . . . One of them.

CONE: He's alone . . . (*walking up to* DEAN) Nice, isn't
he?

PATTY: (*they begin to amble round* DEAN). Nice——

FAK: Cecil Gee——

CONE: Careful not to crush——

PATTY: Pardon.

FAK: Excuse me.

CONE: He don't look very well——

FAK: Bit daft, ain't he?

PATTY: Hi Mister!

25

FAK : Can you hear?

DEAN : (*amazed*). Hey.

PATTY : He's loose.

FAK : He's loony.

CONE : Quack! Quack!

PATTY : Potty!

FAK : Look!

DEAN : What!

CONE : Mmm . . . pooch!

FAK : Boo!

DEAN : Animals——

CONE : Boo! Boo!

DEAN : —Like stampeding——

PATTY : Bim! Bam!

CONE : Bang! Bang!

FAK : (*bringing out his gun*). Yak! Yak! Yak! Yak!

PATTY : Boo boo boo boo.

CONE : Yak! Yak!

DEAN : Control. Control.

FAK : Yak yak yak yak!

PATTY : Tcha! Tcha! Tcha!

FAK : Yay yak yak yak!

PATTY : Tcha tcha tcha tcha!

DEAN : (*making a great effort to collect himself and dominate them*). What are you trying to do?
(CONE *behind* DEAN *gives him a sharp blow at the base of the skull—unseen by the others.*)
Ah!
(DEAN *collapses forward against* FAK *who is sent staggering away firing his gun wildly.* DEAN *falls and is still.*)

FAK : One o' them! One o' them! One o' them!

CONE : Stop.

FAK : . . . Dead . . . he's dead . . . She'll maim me

26

for this. She'll kill me . . .

CONE: Shut up, slob.

FAK: It ain't you. It ain't you. It's me. It's me she'll be after. She said not, not for a bit, not after Aldgate . . . Aldgate . . . Leave it. Come on. Let's leave it. Someone'll take it away— perhaps it'll disappear—perhaps it'll melt. Come on. Let's go. Where'll we go? Let's go to the flicks. Come on, Patty. Let's go.

CONE: Wake up, stupid.

FAK: (*weeping*). It ain't you. It ain't you.

CONE: O blubber shut up.

FAK: It ain't you. It ain't you.

CONE: Oh— (*dismissing it*). Oh—I'll think of something.

FAK: What? . . . What? You—you—yes, you will. That's it, he'll think of something. Yes, you will, you will, you will, oh well. That's well. That'll be all right. That'll be all right.

CONE: Yeah. (*Relaxed and drowsy he picks up the gun and laughs.*)

FAK: What you laughing for?

CONE: He looks a treat.

FAK: A treat . . . A treat . . . a fair treat . . . I feel good . . . I feel bloody good . . . I feel bloody wonderful.

PATTY: (*weeping and laughing*). Mucker! . . . Mucker! . . . Stuck up! . . . That's for you, mucker. You. You. I hate you!

CONE: There's something about this bloke . . . something about the way he looks, he don't look . . . Wonder if he's got a gun. (CONE *finds some American cigarettes in* DEAN's *pocket.*)

27

Yank . . . Is he a yank? . . . Let's get this lot
shifted before someone stumbles over it.

FAK : They got no Yanks.

CONE : Eh?

FAK : They got no Yanks!

CONE : For crying out loud get lifting.

FAK : You'll think of something.

CONE : Yeah.

PATTY : I feel sick.

FAK : Not bad. Not bad eh? . . . Killer! . . . Killer!
. . . Oh! I'm gonna get a whistle sleeker than
this and longer . . . new drains—narrow,
narrow and dark . . . and a new shirt . . . Oh!
White! With French cuffs. And a new tie—and
I'll knot it broad . . . I'm gonna get a
cigarette-holder, thick and stubby. Bamboo
with a gold band.

I'm gonna get me a great red ruby!
Rich and bulging and bold like blood.
Sweet thick pleasure is guttering through me.
Red! Red! Red! 'll make me feel good.

CHORUS : Killer! Killer! Killer!
Killer! Killer! Killer!

FAK : Carry it dressy on a thick gold ring;
Solid and stubby and strong and thick.
Flash 'em in the looker and stab and sting
Send them solid and clutch in the mick.

CHORUS : Killer! Killer! Killer!
Killer! Killer! Killer!

FAK : Sweet old, lovely old, solid gold ruby—
Deep, sweet, blood warm, sombre and soft.
Great sweet pleasure is welling all through
me—
Loose and easy and warm and free.

28

(They are in a state of euphoria or post ecstasy, their minds and nervous system unslung. STEVE *has helped lull them to this.* STEVE *strikes a note.* DEAN *gets up and considers* CONE, FAK *and* PATTY.)*

DEAN : What is this? What is this? I don't get it . . . I like to understand things and I don't understand this . . . It's like some nasty joke . . . it's like spitting in your eye . . . kind of nasty and weak and dangerous . . . If I turn my back on this it'll rot inside me . . . O.K. fellers, this time you won't get me so fast or so easy, we'll wait until the moment I choose and then we'll see who bops who . . .

*(*DEAN *resumes his corpse posture but chooses a different part of the stage to lie down. At a sign from* DEAN, STEVE *strikes a note and wakes the others.)*

FAK : Ah! Hah!

CONE : Eh? What's up with you?

FAK : *(sheepish).* Oh—sorry.

CONE : What you mean sorry?

FAK : Thought it was them. Thought I heard something.

CONE : Nit.

FAK : Might've been them, could've been.

CONE : If you'd heard them.

FAK : Yeah, if I'd heard.

CONE : If. Where'd you think Greta's got to?
(Pause.)

FAK : Greta'll be along.

CONE : I know she'll be along.
(Pause.)

FAK : She'll be along.

29

CONE: She said she'd be here.

FAK: Well . . . (*Pause.*) Here! Where's it gone? Someone's pinched it . . . You've put it somewhere.

PATTY: What's the matter?

FAK: It was here I swear. Oh Gawd!

PATTY: It's there.

FAK: How'd it get there? (*Turning on* CONE.) Very funny, very funny I'm sure. Hah hah.

CONE: Look out! Get that.

(*Enter* DODO. *Apparently about 16 years old with a plain, pale, old face. She might even be an old woman. She wears a man's overcoat too large for her and a big, old hat. She brings on a huge pile of rags, newspapers etc., carrying them, dragging them on a makeshift sledge or pushing them in a pram. She doesn't see the others but she sees the audience and is startled and suspicious. Eventually she decides the best way to get round them is to try and amuse them. She performs any tricks she may know of the simplest, clumsiest kind, making shapes with her fingers resembling animals etc., presently she begins to make noises: clucking, grunting etc., again imitating animals, finally she is at her ease.* PATTY *gets the giggles.*)

PATTY: I wish Maureen could see this.

CONE: Take your tip from me. (*To* DODO) Hiya banana face! What's your name?

(DODO *freezes with fear.*)

DODO: (*inarticulate*). Do . . . do . . . do . . .

CONE: Dodo eh? Hiyah Dodo.

FAK: Hello, Dodo.

CONE: Glad we seen you.

30

PATTY: Ever so glad.

FAK: Ever so glad, eh?

CONE: Because we've got a little present for you.

FAK: A present?

CONE: For her birthday.

FAK: Her birthday?

PATTY: Her birthday.

CONE: A birthday present for her birthday. Let's
show. Let's show her the present.
(CONE *motions them to fetch the* "*body*".)

PATTY: Yes! Yes!

FAK: Yeah!

What'd you guess it was, Dodo? What'd you guess?

PATTY: Guess.

FAK: Guess.

CONE: Guess.

PATTY: Guess. Guess.

CONE: Say something, Dodo. Close your eyes and say
what comes into your eyes. Think! Long and
thin——

FAK: Heavy.

CONE: Yeah. Long and thin and heavy . . . eh, Dodo?

PATTY: Yes.

FAK: Long and thin and heavy.

CONE: What is it? What is it, eh?

PATTY: Long and thin and heavy.

FAK: Long and thin and heavy.

CONE: Long and thin and heavy—like a——?

PATTY: It's like a——

FAK: Like a—— (*Touches* DODO).

DODO: Carpet!

FAK: A carpet!

CONE: A carpet! . . . A carpet . . . Who said this girl
was stupid, eh? . . . Who said she was dull . . .

A carpet. My! What a brain. . . . A carpet. . . .
That's right, Dodo. That's absolutely right.
Clever girl. Well done. All right. Show the lady
her carpet. Look, Dodo! Here's your carpet.
Smashing. Persian.

FAK: A carpet.

CONE: Faky-boy. Show the lady her carpet.

FAK: What?

CONE: (*miming*). You take that. And you take that.

PATTY: This, eh?

FAK: What?

PATTY: That! That!

FAK: Oh . . . that?

CONE: Yes, stupid. Patty, you take this.

PATTY: This? This?

FAK: Oh, I see—that!

CONE: When I say "heave": heave. O.K. One! Two!
Three!——

FAK: (*stumbles against* DODO). Oh pardon.

PATTY: Oh!

CONE: Why, you stupid.

FAK: Oh, I'm ever so sorry.

CONE: You stupid clumsy thing, you. Apologize.
Apologize to Dodo.

FAK: Please excuse me. I'm ever so sorry. Beg
pardon.

CONE: A bit more to you—mind the wrinkle.

FAK: The what?

PATTY: The wrinkle! The wrinkle!

FAK: Oh, the wrinkle.

PATTY: If one of you stood in the middle——

CONE: I'll stand in the middle——

FAK: No. I want to.

CONE: No, I want to.

FAK: No, I want to.

CONE: Oh, very well . . .

PATTY: Take your shoes off.

FAK: What!

PATTY: If you think anything of Dodo you'll take your shoes off before you stand on her nice carpet.

FAK: Oh heck.

CONE: Let's all take our shoes off.

FAK: Oh all right. If we all do.

(CONE, FAK *and* PATTY *remove their shoes.*)

Your feet smell.

CONE: They don't.

FAK: They do.

PATTY: You've got a hole in your sock.

FAK: So's he.

PATTY: Cor! Don't it look silly. What a lark. Why don't you mend it?

CONE: Oh, come on. Let's get out of here.

FAK: What about Greta?

CONE: (*irritated*). Let's get out.

FAK: (*to* DODO). Glad you like the present . . . I said glad you like it . . . What you think about the present, eh? . . . You like it, don't you? . . . Well, go on, say something, it's only polite . . . nice, isn't it? . . . I said it's nice . . . it's nice . . . you do like it, don't you? . . . Go on say you do . . . Go on . . . You do like it, don't you . . . you do, don't you . . . You got to say you do . . . you got to. You got to say you do . . . you do, don't you . . . you do—you do, don't you, you do . . . eh? What? . . . What . . . what . . . what . . . what's the matter? I said what's the matter? . . . Oh . . . oh heck . . . oh hell, oh bloody hell . . . oh bloody bloody . . . look!

33

It's going! It's bloody going! I'm bloody taking it away! Look! Look!

PATTY: What's the matter with him?

FAK: What shall we do with it?

CONE: Wrap it up in brown paper.

FAK: (*seeing* DODO's *pile of old rags*). They'll do.

DODO: No!

FAK: Eh?

DODO: No!

FAK: What!

DODO: No! No!

(FAK *and* DODO, *their joy growing, tussle for the rags.*)

DODO: No! No! No! No! No!

FAK: No! No! No! No! No!

PATTY: (*laughing*). Oh silly, silly Faky-boy. Oh my, isn't it blarney, girl. Oh horrible, horrible.

CONE: My God My God My God My God My God My God My God.

(FAK *lets go the rags and snatches up the newspapers.*)

DODO: Oops!

FAK: Yippee!

(*They stand* DEAN *upright and wrap him in newspapers, winding scotch tape around him to hold the papers in place. Note:* STEVE *may give them the tape, if there seems to be a problem keeping the "body" upright, then* STEVE *may be able to help with commands on his instruments.*)

DODO: No No No No
Throw Throw Throw Throw
So So So So
Blow Blow Blow Blow
Crow Crow Crow Crow

34

Doe Doe Doe Doe.

CONE : What you got there? Sandwiches?

FAK : Strong and neat. That's what I call a packet.
(*Reading a headline from the paper*) "London
policeman beaten by an iron bar." Hurrah!
(FAK *sticks a hat on* DEAN's *head.*)
Got a penny for the guy, Mister! Got a penny
for the guy.
Got a penny for the guy.
Got a penny for the guy.

DODO : Tootle tootle tootle toot.
Tootle tootle tootle toot.

FAK : Got a penny for the guy.
Got a penny for the guy.
(STEVE *picks up the rhythm. The rest pretend to
be playing instruments.*)

DODO : Tootle tootle tootle toot.
Tootle tootle tootle toot.

CONE : Bang Bang Bang Bang.

FAK : Got a penny for the guy.
Got a penny for the guy.

PATTY : Wow wow wow wow
Wow wow wow wow.

DODO : Tootle tootle tootle toot.
Tootle tootle tootle toot.

CONE : Tcha!
(CONE, FAK *and* PATTY *begin to dance round*
DEAN *as round a totem: bellowing words at the
head wrapped in newspaper.*)

PATTY : Wow wow wow wow wow wow wow wow.

FAK : Guy guy guy guy guy guy guy guy.

CONE : Bang bang bang bang bang bang bang bang.
(CONE, FAK *and* PATTY *begin frenziedly to tear
the paper from* DEAN.)

35

CONE: Ah! Ah! Ah! Ah!

FAK: Ah! Ah! Ah! Ah!

PATTY: Ah! Ah! Ah! Ah!

DEAN: Stop.

CONE: (*holding out the American pack*). Cigarette? (DEAN *stretches out his hand and waits.* CONE *puts the cigarette in* DEAN's *hand.* CONE *walks away sulking and angry.*)

DEAN: (*including the audience*). We'll now have a little peace—a little tranquillity. I'm serious. I'm calling a truce for one minute. For one whole minute nobody up here is going to do anything and you can all relax. Nothing's going to happen up here. Nothing at all. (*To the others*) You understand?

PATTY &

FAK: (*in character*). Yes, all right.

DEAN: All right . . . You can just relax. Just let go. O.K.: one minute from now . . . (*After sufficient time, to* DODO) Feeling better? (CONE *rises.*)
That's all right. Time's up.
(*For* DODO.)

Saw a silver feather
Floating in the sun—
Reached up and caught it.
That was one.

Saw a golden nugget
Glitt'ring down below—
Dug deep and found it.
That was two.

Saw a pearly oyster

36

Washed out to sea—
Swam out and fetched it.
That was three.
(CONE *goes as if to exit then, seeing something outside, flattens himself.*)
FAK: (*whispering*). What is it?
CONE: Them.
FAK: Aldgate?
CONE: 'Bout eight of them. All round out there they are.
FAK: Let's have a look.
CONE: Keep back here, you can just—careful! If they see us we won't have a——
FAK: Gawd!
CONE: Where's Greta eh? Where is she? Why ain't she here?
DEAN: Who's out there?
CONE: Never you mind.
DEAN: Friends of yours?
CONE: Yeah, friends of ours. Why don't you go have a little chat?
(*Pause.* DEAN *starts to exit.*)
FAK: They'll smash you.
(*Pause.*)
DEAN: (*to* DODO). Just you wait there, honey. Don't you stir till I come back.
FAK: They'll kill you.
(*Exit* DEAN. CONE, FAK *and* PATTY *watch him outside.*)
Cor!
PATTY: What's happened?
FAK: Cor!
PATTY: Let me see! Let me see!
FAK: Look at that. Will you just look at that.

(FAK *and* PATTY *exit.*)

CONE : What you want to go with him for? Why you want to go with him? Ain't you going to wait for Greta? . . . Greta . . . I'll tell her . . . I'll tell . . . I'll go and find her and tell her . . . tell Greta . . . Greta . . . Mamma! Mamma! Where are you, Mamma? Why you left me? . . . (*Going*) Mamma! (*Off*) Mamma! Greta! . . .
(DODO *plays with the light.* STEVE *starts to tap a rhythm.* DODO *keeps time allowing the sound and the texture of the light to govern her body. Pause.* STEVE *comes to her.*)

STEVE : You're all right. But you let them push you around such a lot. I mean you let them push you around such a lot in the play.
(DODO *looks at him, lights start to come up for interval.* DODO *hastily clears off.*)

(*End of Act One*)

During the interval STEVE *might remain on stage, attending to his instruments, doing odd jobs around the stage, chatting to stage hands etc.*

38

ACT TWO

STEVE *onstage.*
Blackout.
Enter DEAN, PATTY, FAK *and* DODO *who run about the stage with lighted sparklers weaving patterns in the dark.*

DEAN: Ha ha! Whew! Whew!

PATTY: Whew! Whew!

FAK: Ain't it pretty?

PATTY: Christmas! Christmas!

DODO: (*excited*). Oh—oh.

DEAN: Dodo, here. (*He gives* DODO *a sparkler.*)

DODO: Wheesh! Wheesh! Wheesh!

FAK: Watch!

PATTY: Mine's better.

DEAN: Whew! Whew!
(*The last sparkler goes out.*)

PATTY: Aren't there any more?

DEAN: I guess not.

PATTY: Oh . . . quiet, isn't it.

FAK: I see you. (*He grabs at* DODO *who laughs and runs away.*)
(DEAN *laughs.* FAK *laughs uneasily.* FAK *starts to range around the stage.* DEAN, *taking the others, avoids him.*)
Let's have some light, eh? . . . O.K. . . . O.K. . . . Switch on . . . Kill the black . . . I said kill

39

the black . . . D'you hear?

DEAN: (*mocking*). D'you hear?

FAK: What?

DEAN: (*mocking*). What.

FAK: What!

PATTY: (*mocking*). What.

FAK: (*roaring*). Ah! Kill the black! Kill the black!
(FAK *lunges violently around the stage.*)

DODO: (*frightened*). Oh . . . Oh . . .

DEAN: Lights! Lights! (*Lighting a match.*) Let's have
the lights.

PATTY: Switch on. Switch on the lights!

DODO: Lights! Lights! Lights!

DEAN: Lights! Lights!
(*Stage Lights on.*)

FAK: (*to* DEAN). Who d'you think you are? Who
d'you think you are, eh? Want to fight? Want
to fight, eh?

DEAN: You're bigger than me.
(FAK *goes roaring at him.* DEAN *leans sideways
and* FAK *blunders in the wall.* PATTY *laughs and
goes over to* DEAN.)

PATTY: Got a fag? . . . Ta.

FAK: (*to* PATTY). Let's go find the fellers.

PATTY: Not for a bit.

FAK: Come on. Come on.

PATTY: Leave me be. I said not for a bit. They'll be
here soon anyway.

DEAN: Where's—what's his name?

PATTY: You mean Cone?

DEAN: The guy who was here.

PATTY: I expect he's put out . . . well, don't you want
to know why?

DEAN: I guess I know why.

40

PATTY: Oo! You are a one. I guess he's gone to tell——

FAK: Shut up.

PATTY: Who are you talking to? (*To* DEAN) How old are you? I'm twenty-three.

DEAN: (*smiling*). You don't look twenty-three.

PATTY: O—don't I?

DEAN: You're sixteen.

PATTY: Sixteen! Why—why—I'm twenty-three! I'm twenty-three.

(PATTY'*s cigarette has gone out.* DEAN *relights it and then without turning his back on* PATTY, *plays with* DODO.)

FAK: Come on, let's go find the fellers.

PATTY: For heaven's sake.

FAK: Why you flapping over him?

PATTY: I'm not flapping.

FAK: Who is he? What's he doing here?

PATTY: O shut up. Take your nose out of my business. Buzz off.

(FAK *starts to go and then comes back.*)

(*to* DEAN). My favourite colour's true blue, I just love true blue—it's just *the* colour. I've got lots and lots—this is true blue.

DEAN: Yes, I saw it was blue.

PATTY: You're subtle. Oh! I've got lots of true blue—lots and lots. I've even got true blue——

DEAN: What?

PATTY: Nothing.

DEAN: (*smiling*). What were you going to say?

PATTY: Oh, nothing, nothing. What do you like to eat?

DEAN: Oh . . .

PATTY: I think American food, it's—ooh just lovely.

DEAN: You like American food?

PATTY: I've seen it in magazines.

41

DEAN: And Cone's gone to tell who?

FAK: Don't say.

PATTY: Greta.

DEAN: Greta, eh.

PATTY: You needn't bother about her.

FAK: Why! Why needn't he? He'd bloody well better!

PATTY: What do you like to drink?

DEAN: Oh—what do you like?

PATTY: Bourbon.

DEAN: Bourbon!

PATTY: Bourbon on the rocks.

DEAN: My.

FAK: Wipe the grin off your face.

DEAN: Was I smiling?

PATTY: Who asked you to butt in? I thought you'd gone.

FAK: Well I was but then I thought I wouldn't. Do you want to?

PATTY: Not likely. I ain't going west with everything going pop pop and the law and everyone thinking they're General Montgomery.

FAK: Any other time, you'd jump at it.

PATTY: Oh leave me be.

(DEAN, *playing with* DODO, *blows his fingers down one by one.*)

DEAN: Where've they gone? . . . Now where have they gone? . . . Eh! Now you . . . Dear oh dear . . . where can they be?

(PATTY *brings out her home perm outfit.*)

PATTY: I just never will understand this.

DEAN: What have you got there? Why it's a home perm.

PATTY: Do you know about them?

DEAN: Do I know about them? How many times have

42

I watched my sister! Gee! This takes me back.

FAK: What's that for?

DEAN: It's the wave lotion. You curl the hair up in
these—see? And damp it with the wave lotion
. . . and this is the rinse: You put it on to stop
the wave lotion working. You have to be
careful with this stuff. Don't use any metal with
it and don't get it in your eyes or anything.

PATTY: It's awful, isn't it?

DEAN: No, it isn't, it's simple really—when you know
. . . tell you what: I'll help you.

PATTY: O . . . O . . . well thanks—but . . . er . . .

DEAN: Why I'd love to.

FAK: I saw you at the Aldgate bash!

DEAN: Eh?

FAK: 'Swear I saw him there.

PATTY: What are you getting at?

FAK: You was there, wasn't you?

DEAN: No . . . what was the Aldgate bash?

FAK: Go on! Don't you read the papers?
(DEAN *shrugs his shoulders*.)
You missed something. There was a lovely
photo of some of our lot after that.

PATTY: Stupid, getting their faces about.

FAK: Bottles and razors all down the Commercial
road just as the flicks were coming out. And a
lonely copper clapped in his daisy. Cor! You
should've seen him. One eye hanging out and
his nose all over the side of his face, he wasn't
half slammed. Coo! They hung it on him—and
funny thing—you had to laugh: he said he was
getting married next day.

PATTY: (*excited*). Oh . . . Oh . . .

FAK: Take you some time.

43

PATTY: They're always after the Aldgate lot.

FAK: Yeah. They're our regulars.

DEAN: Do they come and fight you back?

FAK: We get plenty of warning.

PATTY: They daren't.

FAK: Yeah. That was a real good do—some of their chaps'll never walk straight again . . . one of our lot lost a finger.

DEAN: (*sickened*). Oh.
(*Long pause.*)

PATTY: Aren't you bored? I'm bored.

FAK: We could go to the flicks.

PATTY: What's on?

FAK: Anybody got a paper?
(DODO *holds out one of hers.*)

DEAN: Sixth of March.

FAK: Ava Gardner. (*Or other, Author's note*) At the Dominion—I think. . . . Let's get a guy and go collecting . . . money in it.

DEAN: Where'd you get a guy?

PATTY: (*catty*). Dodo'd do.

DEAN: Let's perm Patty!

PATTY: What!

DEAN: Let's perm you, Patty. Where's Patty's perm?

PATTY: Go on, it'd look ever so silly.

DEAN: (*charming her*). Monsieur Dean! Coiffeur des dames.

PATTY: Well—so long as you're sure it'll be all right.

DEAN: Yippee! Catch! Curlers? Mug?

STEVE: I'll get you a mug. (*He exits and returns with a mug.*)

DEAN: Lotion? Thanks.

PATTY: It's here.

DEAN: Cast it in . . . anybody got a comb?

44

FAK: Yes.

PATTY: Is it clean?

DEAN: Of course it's clean—no. Mine's cleaner.

PATTY: Thanks, we'll use mine.

DEAN: Cotton wool?

FAK: There's some here.

DEAN: O.K. Fak! Seat for the lady. Dodo, you hold this paper and read. Can you read? Atta girl! Fak: mug and cotton. Patty: papers and curlers. All ready? Good. Now, get this:

DODO: Divide . . .

DEAN: Divide?

DODO: Divide scalp into three sections: from ear to ear and down centre back. See fig. 4.

PATTY: Be careful.

DEAN: Scalp in three sections from ear to ear and down centre back. O.K.?

FAK: O.K.

DODO: Take a section the size of a curler.

DEAN: Curler.

PATTY: Curler.

DODO: Thoroughly saturate with the lotion.

DEAN: Lotion.

FAK: Lotion.

DODO: Fold an end paper over and under.

DEAN: End paper.

PATTY: One of these?

DEAN: Yip! Like this, see?

FAK: That?

DEAN: Ya.

PATTY: Just a minute ——

DEAN: Faster there——

DODO: Wind it firmly to the root of the hair.

DEAN: Wind it firmly to the root of the hair. Patty,

45

you're going to look lovely.

PATTY: I hope so I'm sure.

DEAN: O.K. More. More.

PATTY: Mind you do it proper.

DEAN: Leave it to us. Now: let's have a system.

PATTY: Take a section the size of a curler.

DEAN: Take a section the size of a curler.

PATTY: Thoroughly saturate with the lotion.

FAK: Thoroughly saturate with the lotion.

PATTY: Fold an end paper over and under.

DODO: Fold an end paper over and under.

PATTY: Wind it firmly to the root of the hair.

DEAN: Wind it firmly to the root of the hair . . .
Again!

PATTY: Take a section the size of a curler.

DEAN:
DODO: } Take a section the size of a curler.
FAK:

PATTY: Thoroughly saturate with the lotion.

DEAN:
DODO: } Thoroughly saturate with the lotion.
FAK:

PATTY: Fold an end paper over and under.

DEAN:
DODO: } Fold an end paper over and under.
FAK:

PATTY: Wind it firmly to the root of the hair.

DEAN:
DODO: } Wind it firmly to the root of the hair.
FAK:

DEAN: Take a section the size of a curler
DODO: Thoroughly saturate with the lotion
PATTY: Fold an end paper over and under
& FAK: Wind it firmly to the root of the hair.

46

DEAN : Again!
DEAN :⎤ Take a section the size of a curler
DODO : | Thoroughly saturate with the lotion
PATTY : ⎰ Fold an end paper over and under
& FAK :⎦ Wind it firmly to the root of the hair.

       Take a section
       Saturate
       Fold a paper
       Wind it firm.

DEAN : When the curls are fully *wound.*
PATTY :⎱
DODO : ⎰ Section.
& FAK :
DEAN : Sit fifteen minutes out of *draughts.*
PATTY :⎱
DODO : ⎰ Saturate.
& FAK :
DEAN : After that take out a *test* curl.
PATTY :⎱
DODO : ⎰ Paper.
& FAK :
DEAN : See the curl is strong and well *formed.*
PATTY :⎱
DODO : ⎰ Wind.
& FAK :
DEAN : If the test wave's weak and *poor.*
PATTY :⎱
DODO : ⎰ Sec.
& FAK :
DEAN : Take a look at figure five. (My! It is poor).
PATTY :⎱
DODO : ⎰ Sat.
& FAK :
DEAN : Curl the curl again and *leave.*

47

PATTY :
DODO : } Pap.
& FAK :

DEAN : A few more minutes, then unwind.

　　　　/　　　/　　　/
DEAN : Careful not to sit in draughts.
FAK :　　　　Sec.
DODO :　　　　　　　Sat.
PATTY :　　　　　　　　　　Pap.
FAK :　　　　　　　　　　　　　Wind.

　　　/　　/　　　/　　　/　　　/
FAK : Use no metal with the lotion.
DODO :　　　　Sec.
PATTY :　　　　　　Sat.
DEAN :　　　　　　　　　Pap.
DODO :　　　　　　　　　　　Wind.

　　　　/　　　/　　　/
DODO : May be set in many styles (See note attached).
PATTY :　　　　Sec.
DEAN :　　　　　　　Sat.
FAK :　　　　　　　　　Pap.
PATTY :　　　　　　　　　　　Wind.
(*The scene, while remaining light-hearted,*
becomes riotous.)

DODO : Saturate. Saturate. Saturate. Saturate.
DEAN : } Sec sat pap wind!
PATTY : } Sec sat pap wind!
& FAK :

DODO : Lots of lotion lots of lotion!
PATTY : } Sec sat pap wind!
& FAK : } Sec sat pap wind!

DEAN : Pour the rinse in! Pour the rinse in!
DEAN : } Pour the rinse in! Pour the rinse in!
PATTY : } Sec! Sat! Sick! Sock! Pip! Pap!
& FAK : } Pop! Pup! Pep! Pump! Pimp! Pamp! Wind!

48

(*Enter* CONE. DODO *pours the rinse into the mug of lotion.*)

PATTY : She's put the rinse in the lotion.

DEAN : (*laughing*). Ah—! Oh dear! Oh dear me! Oh dear me! Oh dear! Oh—you shouldn't have done that. Oh dear . . . What's it say here? After fifteen minutes rinse . . . Oh dear . . .

FAK : Smells terrible.

PATTY : It's gone green.

FAK : Let's pour it on and see what happens.

PATTY : What!

DEAN : She'd go bald. How'd you like a wig, Patty?

PATTY : Thanks very much.

DEAN : Fak'll spit on you.

FAK : Looks like it'd melt sixpence.

DODO : Let's try.

PATTY : Don't waste sixpence.

DEAN : You could blind somebody with this.

CHORUS : That's an idea.

(CONE *laughs gently.*)

PATTY : Go on. Laugh. Have a good giggle. Very funny I'm sure. What about me? What about me? I'm laughing myself silly. Look at me. Look! I'll look wonderful won't I? A real treat. You make me sick. Look at it. Look at it. It's all mucked up. Ugh! It's horrible.

(DODO *tries to help her.*)

Ugh! Get away. Don't touch me you nasty little thing. Leave me be. Leave me be.

DEAN : Oh, Patty, you can wash it.

CHORUS : Wash! Wash! It's chemical and it needs chemical to get it off—and the chemical's there—ruined. All it's good for is blinding people. Oh, you're so stupid. I wish I'd never set eyes on you. . . .

49

I wish I was at home all nice and quiet in bed.

DEAN: Oh, Pat, it was a lot of fun, wasn't it?

PATTY: Very funny for you, I'm sure.

DEAN: Tell you what! I'll buy you a new perm. Come on, let's go and get it washed, eh?

(DEAN *sees* CONE *move as if to stop him leaving. Exit* PATTY. *Pause. Re-enter* PATTY.)

PATTY: There's something out there—big and funny—I felt it go past me in the dark.

CONE: Let's dress up as guys and go collecting.

FAK: What?

CONE: Let's dress up as guys.

FAK: What for?

CHORUS: Let's dress up.

FAK: Cor break my bleeding heart! We got to dress up? (*To* PATTY.) What you shivering for?

PATTY: It's Greta. It's Greta.

FAK: What you mean it's Greta?

PATTY: It's Greta, there's something funny going on.

FAK: Something funny?

PATTY: It's Greta.

CONE: (*to* DEAN). What you say, Yank?
(*Pause.*)

DEAN: Very well.

FAK: Oh well, what junk for me. What dress? There's not enough here for five.

PATTY: There is.

FAK: How many are there? One, two, three, four, five. There's not enough for five people.

PATTY: 'Course there's enough for five—Dodo's dressed up anyway.

(*They start to cover themselves from head to foot with the old coats and blankets, masking their faces and covering their heads.*)

50

CONE: Please to remember
ALL: Please to remember
Please to remember
Please to remember the fifth of November.

Please to remember
Please to remember
Please to remember the fifth of November.
(*Enter* GRETA *dressed as the others. She mingles with them unnoticed.*)
Please to remember
Please to remember
Please to remember the fifth of November
Please to remember the fifth of November
Gunpowder, treason and plot.
(*All six are strung out across the stage.*)
DODO: (*in terror, her hat falling off*). There are six . . . there are six . . . Oh! . . . Oh! . . . Oh!
DEAN: All right honey, it's me, Dean, I'm here.
(DEAN *goes to* DODO, *the others reform so that their identity is confused.* DEAN *is at first guarded, then as he gets more confident, almost contemptuous; but after he fails to unmask* GRETA *he loses his psychological balance and the others can get at him.*)
CONE: Dean.
DEAN: Yes?
CONE: That your name, Dean?
DEAN: Yeah.
FAK: Dean.
PATTY: Dean.
CONE: Where you from, Dean?
DEAN: The U.S.
PATTY: What part of the U.S.?

51

DEAN: New York.

PATTY: (*impressed*). New York!

FAK: Do you know Pampinato?

DEAN: Pampinato? Who's he.

CONE: Where d'you live in New York, Dean?

DEAN: Where do I live!

FAK: Where d'you live?

DEAN: I have an apartment.

CONE: An apartment.

PATTY: An apartment.

DEAN: I share an apartment.

CONE: Share.

PATTY: Share.

DEAN: This is very stupid, very stupid. Cone, for heaven's sake, take off that silly mask.

GRETA: (*speaking with an Australian accent*). Who d'you share your apartment with, Dean?

DEAN: Uh?

(*As he turns to the unfamiliar voice* CONE *moves across his vision.* PATTY *speaks behind him,* GRETA *changes her position.*)

PATTY: Who d'you share with?

DEAN: A friend.

CONE: Who? . . . What's his name?

PATTY: Afraid?

FAK: Afraid to get mixed up?

DEAN: This is stupid! Stupid!

FAK: You're trying to put us off.

PATTY: You're afraid to tell us.

CONE: Is there any harm in telling us?

DEAN: Of course there's no harm.

PATTY: Then why not tell us?

DEAN: This is a stupid situation.

CONE: Is this a stupid situation?

52

FAK: You know Petticoat Lane?

DEAN: What else?

FAK: Nice district Aldgate.

DEAN: I wouldn't know.

FAK: Petticoat Lane is in Aldgate.

DEAN: Why don't you go play Guy Fawkes?

CONE: Who shares your apartment?

DEAN: Conrad.

PATTY: Con——

FAK: Con——

CONE: Conrad who?

DEAN: Scaeffer.

CONE: Conrad Scaeffer.

PATTY: Who else do you know?

CONE: Who else are your friends?

PATTY: Have you any friends?

DEAN: Have I any friends?

FAK: Who else?

CONE: Name them.

DEAN: Clive West, Mary Allen, Zachary Hope, Alma——

CONE: Why not give the real names?

PATTY: The real names.

FAK: The people you really go around with.

DEAN: This is idiotic, fantastic.

FAK: Gringo!

GRETA: Pivesky!

FAK: Turps!

CONE: Pampinato!

DEAN: I don't know them.

PATTY: Why should you know them?

CONE: What reason have you to know them?

FAK: Did we say you did?

(By an effort of concentration, and by identifying

53

the voices, DEAN *has eliminated* PATTY, FAK *and* CONE, *now he tries to get hold of* GRETA.)

DEAN: You! You! Who——?

(GRETA *has slipped away,* DEAN *finds* CONE.)

CONE: Who's Scaeffer?

DEAN: Journalist?

PATTY: What paper?

DEAN: I—I——

PATTY: Showgirl—Mary Allen?

DEAN: No—a——

GRETA: What?

DEAN: Stenographer.

PATTY: Who for?

DEAN: Men in shoes—in a shoe company.

CONE: Name?

DEAN: How should I know? I don't——

FAK: Pampinato.

DEAN: What?

CONE: Know that name?

DEAN: I—I heard it.

CONE: So you heard it!

GRETA: Your mother was born in——?

DEAN: Sure—I mean Detroit.

GRETA: Sure?

DEAN: Sure I'm sure.

CONE: Absolutely sure?

DEAN: Why not! Why not!

PATTY: Brothers!

DEAN: Brothers!

FAK: Brothers.

CONE: Brothers.

DEAN: Brothers, brothers my mother was born in . . .

CONE: Pampinato!

DEAN: Yes?

54

CONE: You seen him.

DEAN: I——

PATTY: Your friends——

FAK: They'll get you into trouble.

PATTY: Catch me out. Catch! Catch!

DEAN: No.

GRETA: Who's Mary Pivesky?

CONE: You know her.

PATTY: Gringo.

DEAN: Who? Who?

FAK: Don't know him?

DEAN: Not said——

CONE: The shoemaker——

DEAN: What?

PATTY: You deny——

DEAN: Shoe? Shoe?

PATTY: Said you——

FAK: —Get it out——

PATTY: Say you——

DEAN: No shoe——

PATTY: Said——

FAK: Get——

CONE: Get——

GRETA: Mother born Pittsburgh.

DEAN: Mamma!

(*Climax.* DEAN *would be finished but* GRETA *has lost interest and moves away, possibly to talk to* STEVE, *the focus of action seems to go with her.*)

CONE: Lepstein.

FAK: You know him.

CONE: He's a friend of yours.

PATTY: Say Gringo.

CONE: Know him?

FAK: Shoemaker.

55

PATTY : Liar.

CONE : You're lying.

FAK : Who's—Who's——

CONE : Who's Zachary Hope?

PATTY : You won't tell us.

FAK : You're afraid.

CONE : You're afraid.

FAK : What are you afraid of?

PATTY : Afraid.

CONE : Afraid to tell.

FAK : Tell us.

PATTY : Tell.

CONE : Stop . . . Notice something?
(*Pause.*)

FAK : No one's talking.

CONE : That's right . . . No one's talking . . . Why you
not talking, Dean? . . . You know? . . . he
thinks we're stupid.

FAK : Stupid?

CONE : Look at his face. Look at his face. We make
him sick. "Take off that silly mask, Cone, you
make me sick."

FAK : Make him talk!

PATTY : Talk!

CONE : Where's Dodo? Where's the little bitch? Come
here! Come here! Gotcha! All right Dodo: tell
Dean to talk. Tell your friend to speak.

DODO : Speak.

CONE : Louder Dodo, louder.

DODO : Speak. Speak.
(DEAN *lunges at* CONE *who instinctively gives
way,* DEAN *seizes* DODO *and holds her.*)

CONE : (*screaming*). Answer. Answer. Answer.

FAK : Sock.

56

PATTY : Smash.

CONE : Why won't you answer?

DEAN : Because I won't submit to this degradation.

FAK : Eh?

CONE : Degradation!

PATTY : (*losing control, a howl from the depths*).
Yawooerl.

CONE : Yoweeoch. Yoweeoch.

PATTY : Yawooerl. Yawooerl. Ugh! Ugh!

FAK : Whaow. Aherooigh. Aherooigh.
(*Screaming with anger and frustration* PATTY,
FAK *and* CONE *fall upon* DEAN. FAK *raises his gun
to club* DEAN. GRETA, *a schoolmaster's cane in
her hand, strikes something sharply.*)

GRETA : Stop.

FAK : Eh?

GRETA : (*quietly*). Drop it.
(FAK *drops the gun.* GRETA *gently knocks* FAK,
CONE *and* PATTY *aside. As she approaches* DEAN
*he takes up the mug of rinse. She stretches out
her hand and waits.* DEAN *puts it into her hand,
she drinks and smashes the mug.*)

DEAN : My.
(GRETA *divests herself of part of her disguise.
Her hair is long, straight and red, falling from
her brow like a Japanese lion wig. Her face is
very heavily made up and almost dead white. She
catches up the corner of the blanket she is
wearing and loops it over her arm to give herself
a swashbuckling air.*)
My.
(CONE *goes to* GRETA *and plays following scene
touching her hair, her hand, her arm.*)

GRETA : (*lazily*). What's been doing, eh? Up? Cooking?

57

Where did the gun come from?

CONE: Fak.

(*An atmosphere of threat emanates from* GRETA. *Pause.*)

FAK: Well, I give it you. (*He is very frightened.*) I was going to give it you. (*Pause.*) I was.

CONE: Got it off his old man.

(*Pause.*)

GRETA (*waving* FAK *away with the cane*). No guns.

(FAK *very depressed retires well out of reach.*)

(*to* CONE). Mind my hair.

CONE: (*privileged*). Sorry.

GRETA: You're a drag.

CONE: (*knowing she doesn't mean it*). And what else?

GRETA: What's that?

CONE: Fireworks.

GRETA: You're kidding me.

CONE: Yes they are.

GRETA: Well well, what'll you lot get up to next? Fireworks. Well, I s'pose even he (FAK) is safe with a sparkler. Hey, move over.

CONE: No you.

GRETA: (*good humoured*). No you. Go on, move over.

CONE: Oh!

GRETA: Well, I told you. What else has been happening?

CONE: He turned up.

GRETA: Oh yes, him. (*She heaves herself round to stare at* DEAN *who stares back. After a while she turns away but remains very conscious of him.*) Mm . . . Well what else have you been up to? Come on tell me, tell me about the fireworks.

CONE: Fak found 'em, he knocked them off a lorry.

GRETA: Fak's had a busy day Fak has.

58

CONE: Was standing outside a caff not far from Hendon Central, driver'd gone in for a cuppa, and we just happened to be there having a chat, and I saw the lorry didn't have no driver. O.K. I says to Fak, now your chance, and so while I keeps a look out—you know the way I can so no one notices—he heaved himself up over the side in no time and then what do you think . . . well?

GRETA: (*her mind on* DEAN) Mm?

CONE: Oh.

(*Long pause.* GRETA *laughs gently.* CONE *goes round the stage banging and breaking things.* GRETA *takes no notice.*)

CONE: What about me? What about me?

GRETA: What about you? This about you.

(GRETA *beats* CONE *up in an easy, lazy, rather splendid manner. He gives himself up in a sort of ecstasy. When she has done he lies relaxed and peaceful.*)

DEAN: (*sickened*). North. South. East. West. Foot kicks face and mouth bites belly. Kiss me Jock, that's right.

GRETA: Eh? . . . Oh are you still here?

DEAN: My God.

GRETA: Where did you say your mother came from? (*Before* DEAN *can answer she has turned her attention to the others.*)

GRETA: (*cheerily*). What a lot! What a mess! What a look out eh? Right! Wake up! Look lively! Jump to it! Show a leg there! Right! When I come into the room stand up! Good morning.

PATTY
& FAK: Eh? What?

CONE: Morning! Morning!

PATTY
& FAK: Morning Miss.

GRETA: Good morning. Stand up! Right! Sit down!

CONE: Please Miss I've got a pain in my leg.

GRETA: (*beating him*). No excuses.

CONE: Yaooer! Yaooer!

FAK: Please Miss, here's an apple.

GRETA: Thanks boy, back to your place. (*To audience*) Wake up! Wake up! Right! Maps! Blackboard! Chalk!

FAK: Please Miss may I be excused?

GRETA: No, stay behind and fill up the inkwells. If a herring and a half cost four farthings?

PATTY: Sevenpence please Miss.

GRETA: Right! Come to the top. (*To audience*) Pay attention! I shall get to you in a minute. Right! In fourteen hundred and ninety-two——

DEAN: (*almost unconsciously automatic reply*). Columbus sailed the ocean blue.

GRETA: Wrong. King Alfred burnt the cakes. (*To* FAK) Spell Miscellaneous.

PATTY: M—I—S—S—er . . . er . . .

GRETA: Right! Right! Right! Write it on the blackboard. (*To* FAK) Hey! What's that?

FAK: Please Miss, nothing Miss, it's a note, Miss.

GRETA: Let me see. Oo! You wicked boy, go wash your hands this instant.
(PATTY, FAK *and* CONE *have gone wild, laughing, playing, somersaulting, etc.*)

GRETA: (*to audience*). Right, you! Two and three-quarters from five and five-eighths? Kings and Queens of England from George the first *backwards*? Battle of Botany Bay? Wrong!

60

Wrong! Wrong!
(GRETA *is madly waving her cane around and
now gets it in her eye. She roars and bellows
with pain, clutching her eye.*)
DEAN : What is it? What's wrong? Can I help? Please
let me—let me have a look. Is it bad?
(GRETA *now blubbering in a hurt and shaken
fashion allows him to look at her eye. But once
he's doing it he finds himself looking into an eye
that's looking right back at him. She begins to
rumble with amusement.* DEAN *draws back, not
knowing whether she was teasing him. The
others laugh with her. Presently the laughter
subsides. Pause.*)
GRETA :   What you doing sailor boy?
What you doing sailor love?
What you doing ship ahoy?
What you doing little dove?

What you doing little monkey?
What you doing little donkey?
What you doing little fancy?
What you doing little love?
(*Pause. Her feeling of good humour is reflected
by* FAK, CONE *and* PATTY. *Suddenly but subtly*
GRETA's *feeling changes, she is listening.* CONE
too starts to listen.)
FAK : What is it? What's the matter?
CONE : Ssh.
(*Pause.*)
GRETA : (*not very excited*). Hear it?
CONE : (*rather tense*). Yeah.
(CONE *goes and looks out.*)
GRETA : Well?

61

CONE: I don't know.
      (*He goes again, this time right off. Pause.*)
FAK: Yeah, now I can hear it.
PATTY: What is it eh?
FAK: Listen.
PATTY: I can't hear nothing . . . we going to find our
       lot eh? Our fellers?
FAK: Dunno.
PATTY: Eh? Eh?
FAK: I dunno.
      (*Pause. Re-enter* CONE.)
CONE: There's something on.
GRETA: What d'you mean?
CONE: I don't know.
GRETA: (*languid*). Well——
CONE: Shall I get the others?
GRETA: Well—
        (*Pause.*)
CONE: I don't like it, let's get the others.
GRETA: O.K., why not?
CONE: You coming?
GRETA: Me?
CONE: Yes.
GRETA: I don't think I'll come.
CONE: Why? Why not?
GRETA: Don't think I'll come, think I'll have a bit of a
       nap.
CONE: A nap.
GRETA: Yeah a bit of a sleep. (*To* FAK) You going. Not
       her.
PATTY: I want to. I want to.
GRETA: Harrow Road, yes? You first.
        (*She listens then motions* FAK *and* PATTY *to go.*
        Exit FAK *and* PATTY.)

CONE: Where'll you nap?

GRETA: Oh . . . here . . . ain't you going?

CONE: He's not for you . . . not for you . . . is he?

GRETA: See you later . . . see you here.

CONE: Is he?

GRETA: Oh get off.

> (*Pause. Exit* CONE. GRETA *turns slowly and sleepily, is seen to be pregnant. Sees* DEAN *watching her.*)
>
> Oh yes, you. . . . Mm . . .
>
> (*She rises and exits slowly.*)

DEAN: What's going on here?

STEVE: Search me.

> (*The lights fade, house lights coming up. Exit* DEAN, STEVE *and* DODO.)

(*End of Act Two*)

ACT THREE

An hour or so later.
Dark stage.
STEVE *playing a terrible noise.*

DEAN : (*off*). Dodo! Dodo! Dodo!
　　　(*Noise. Enter* CONE.)
　CONE : (*to* STEVE). Where's Greta?
STEVE : Don't know.
　CONE : Fight! Fight! It's a fight! Out! Out! Out!
　　　There! Got it? A gang fight! Pampinato!
　　　Aldgate! Bang! Bang! (*To the audience*)
　　　Crackle! Crackle! Behind you! Behind you!
　　　Behind your head! Turn your head—what's
　　　behind? What? What?—As you turn your
　　　head—on your neck! Neck! Feel it! Too dark
　　　to see but there's something behind—feel it!
　　　Can you smell something. Can you? Can you
　　　smell it? Breath! What is it? What you
　　　breathing, breathing in, in, into yourself? Can
　　　you breathe? Can you? Can you breathe? Ah!
　　　Ah! You can't! You can't breathe! You can't!
　　　Ah! Ah!
　　　(*Enter* PATTY *running,* CONE *catches her by her*
　　　coat and swings her round and round, letting her
　　　go and catching her again.)
　PATTY : (*screaming*). Ah! Ah! Ah!

64

CONE: (*laughing*). Ha, ha. Done! Done! Hah hah.
(CONE *lets go her coat and is himself flung
offstage by the momentum. Silence. Pause.*)
PATTY: (*screaming almost soundlessly*). Fak! Fak! Fak!
Fak!
(*Pause. Enter* DODO *blind and blundering, she
bumps into* PATTY *and clutches her.*)
PATTY: (*a screaming whisper*). No! No! Ugh! Go away!
Agh! Agh!
(DODO *clings to* PATTY *who tries to scrape her
off, both consumed with terror and hysteria.*)
DODO: Oh—oh—oh——
PATTY: No! Don't touch me! Agh! Agh!
(*This encounter goes on for a while and against
it rises a drumming sequence, or sequence of
intense, rhythmical, complicated noise. Finally*
PATTY *exits and* DODO *crawls under some rags,
but the noise continues.*)
DEAN: (*off*). Dodo! Dodo! Where are you? Dodo!
(*Enter* DEAN.)
Dodo! Dodo!
(DODO *burrows deeper under the rags, the
movement catches* DEAN's *eye.*)
Dodo . . . Look! I've got something for you . . .
Look Dodo, look it's me, you're all right with
me . . . it's me, don't be afraid, don't be afraid
Dodo . . . I'm strong and I understand . . . it's
terrible, terrible to be weak to try and bear the
terror pressing in on your imagination . . . each
moment as it passes is a moment won from
fear of being hurt . . . but what if they should
come tonight? What if they should get you
tonight? Or tomorrow . . . or next week . . .
and when the moment comes . . . when they

65

get you . . . oh Dodo! I understand, I understand your fear. There's no loving trust that I
withhold from you. Every privilege of my
strength I share with you. There, there.
(*Pause.*)

STEVE: What's happened to your hand?

DEAN: Oh, I don't know, it got burnt, something burnt
it out there. I don't know.
(STEVE *gets something to treat the hand.*)
There. There, that's all right. I'm here, nothing
can happen now. They can't hurt you now.
(STEVE *returns and starts dressing the hand.*)

DEAN: This makes me so angry, so angry—all this.
(*Enter* CONE.)

CONE: (*to* DEAN). Where is she?

DEAN: Who?

CONE: Where? Where is she?

DEAN: Greta?

CONE: Where is she?

DEAN: How should I know? What do you want with
her? She can look after herself I guess.

CONE: (*to* STEVE). You seen her?

STEVE: No.

DEAN: My God, this mess, this waste, this viciousness.

STEVE: Why be angry?

DEAN: Why be angry? Why be angry? It concerns me!
It concerns me! I'm part of the human race and
this waste—this violence—this degradation—it
betrays humanity, it betrays mankind. That's
why I'm angry. Thanks, I can manage by
myself. If people will only have patience and
intelligence and will power there's nothing we
can't master and control. All this mess, this
filth—and it's not us who suffer, not us, not

66

the strong ones—people like that woman, they don't suffer—no, it's this child. What a responsibility they have, people like her: self-respect, self-discipline, love, decency, mutual trust, all gone, the things weaker people can build their lives on, live in peace and security. Mutual social laws, the bedrock you can build your happiness on. And it's our responsibility: people like you and me and her. In all humility we have to carry the world, we have to educate and love—but when I think of that woman: loose, vicious, destructive——

CONE: Hey! . . . You!

DEAN: Yes?

CONE: After I left . . .

DEAN: Well?

CONE: You know when I mean——

DEAN: I'm afraid I don't.

CONE: You know when I mean—after I left—here—a bit ago—you were left with her—alone—Well, what happened?

DEAN: What do you mean what happened?

CONE: What did you do?

DEAN: What did we do?

CONE: What did you do together?

DEAN: Nothing.

CONE: Nothing?

DEAN: No.

CONE: Go on! . . . Go tell us another. That's right. Thousands'd believe you.

DEAN: I'm telling you the truth.

CONE: Rubbish. (*Pause.*) What's the time?

DEAN: You've got a watch.

CONE: Yeah but it's stopped.

67

DEAN: Why not put it right?

STEVE: One ten.

CONE: Oh well, she won't be long then will she?
(*Enter* FAK.)
Seen her?

FAK: Ain't she here?

CONE: No.

FAK: She'll be about.

CONE: Go and look for her. Go back the Regal, down the green.

FAK: What me?

CONE: Yes.

FAK: Why don't you go?

CONE: Said I'd see her here.

FAK: I'm tired.

CONE: Said I'd see her.

FAK: You go, I'll wait. Cor there's a bimp out there —millions, well hundreds, thought I saw Pampinato, that give me a turn.

DEAN: Who's out there?

FAK: Who's out there!

DEAN: Aldgate?

FAK: Who else?

CONE: Where's Patty?

FAK: . . . Oh Gawd . . . I lost her . . . I lost Patty . . . Where she got to? Forgot all about her I did till you mentioned . . . Where's Patty? got excited with the bashing and . . . forgot her . . .

CONE: Go and look for her.

FAK: Yeah, yeah. I better hadn't I?

CONE: Back of the Regal, down the green.

FAK: Think she'll be there?

CONE: She'll be there—and if you see Greta——

FAK: Yeah?

CONE : Bring her back here.

FAK : See me bring her back!

CONE : Well, tell her! Tell her!

FAK : Yeah, O.K. O.K.

(*Exit* FAK. *Pause.*)

DEAN : (*to* DODO). How you feeling eh? Better? Ready to face the world? No, no, don't hide your head . . . don't hide. You've got to face fear Dodo, you've got to face evil, otherwise it gets bigger and bigger, not looking at it, pretending it's not there—if you run away from evil—no you've got to fight it back, and you've got to make yourself strong, strong and clever, stupidity is a sin, a sin Dodo, because if you're stupid you can't see the evil in the world, and you can't fight it effectively . . . Oh Dodo, am I asking too much? Nothing, then, nothing, you just lean on me.

(*Pause.*)

CONE : You swear nothing happened?

DEAN : Yes.

(*Pause.*)

CONE : (*to* STEVE). Got any dice?

STEVE : Dice? Can get you some.

CONE : O.K.

(STEVE *exits. Pause. Re-enters with dice which* CONE *takes and starts throwing, getting more violent.*)

DEAN : Must you make such a racket?

CONE : What?

DEAN : You're making a lot of noise.

CONE : Why not? Why shouldn't I?

DEAN : This child's asleep.

CONE : So bloody what?

69

DEAN: Stop that!

CONE: Shut your cakehole.

DEAN: Stop that.

CONE: Get knotted.

> (DEAN *rises*. CONE *picks up a weapon, likewise*
> DEAN. *They face each other across the stage*.)

CONE: Don't you come near me . . . I know your
kind, judo—toss you a mile . . . If you come
near me I'll bash you.

> (*Pause.* DODO *blubbering quietly*.)

What you doing here? Who are you?

DEAN: Don't frighten the child.

CONE: Like hell I won't—Why you hanging round eh?

DEAN: We've been through that.

CONE: And got nowhere.

DEAN: You tried hard enough.

CONE: Get back—Look, stop talking, stop going on. I
don't give—look, just get out, go away, go
away, go away and get lost. Before she comes
back.

DEAN: That woman?

CONE: Don't ask any questions, don't talk, just go,
get out, go.

DEAN: Like hell I will.

> (*Pause*.)

CONE: What happened after I'd gone?

DEAN: I told you.

CONE: What happened?

DEAN: I'm not telling you again.

> (*Pause*.)

CONE: Maybe it's all right then eh? Maybe it's all
right?

DEAN: So little self-respect. So little self-control.

> (*Enter* FAK *panting and carrying* PATTY.)

What's the matter? What's happened?

FAK : Found her, she'd fainted, up by Church Street she was.

CONE : Seen Greta?

FAK : Who? No. What'll we do eh? What'll we do?

DEAN : Where's Steve? Steve!

STEVE : Eh?

FAK : Don't shout. It's crawling with them outside—millions of them—well, lots. Had an 'orrible time coming back, bent double I was most the way—cor she's a fair weight, she don't look it but my she's heavy.

(PATTY *beginning to come round.* CONE *starts to throw dice, gently, but unhappily.*)

PATTY : Oh . . . oh . . . oh . . .

DEAN : There, that's all right, you're all right now.

FAK : We're here.

PATTY : Oh . . . oh I want to hide, I want to disappear.

DEAN : There, there.

FAK : There, there.

PATTY : I feel sick.

FAK : You going to be sick?

PATTY : No, it's all right.

DEAN : Put this round you.

FAK : (*taking off his jacket*). Here, let her have mine. What happened to you?

PATTY : What happened to you?

FAK : I dunno.

DEAN : Never mind that now, how you feeling?

PATTY : Oh, better than I was . . . oh it was awful. All alone in the dark, I never been alone in the dark before, not in the real dark . . . I never been really alone in the dark ever. (*Starting to cry again.*)

71

(CONE *begins to throw his dice with more violence*.)

FAK : (*holding* PATTY *and comforting her, she gradually quietens*). There, there.

PATTY : Is it all right to keep this a bit?

FAK : Yeah.

PATTY : It's nice talking.

FAK : Yeah.

PATTY : All friendly and warm.

FAK : Yeah.

PATTY : Perhaps I was stupid—just stupid—made it all up eh? Just silly! Silly! Nothing at all, nothing, and there was I all scared of nothing.

FAK : Yeah.

PATTY : Oh no it weren't nothing, I know it weren't.

FAK : Cor did you see them? Did you? Thousands— well dozens. Where'd they all come from? Oh he's been at it, Pampinato has, Pampinato's been about—where's the police I'd like to know, where's the bloody coppers?

(DEAN *takes up the dice and throws them*.)

Pacing the area they was coshing the lot, blimey! And back of the Regal—fair made your hair curl, that noisy. And some feller hanging from a lamp-post—

(CONE *takes up the dice and throws them*.)

coshing them from above—whack! With a bottle. And they grabbed the post and chucked him in the canal, lamp an' all.

(CONE *and* DEAN *are throwing the dice alternately*.)

What you playing for eh? Three five. What's the stakes? Two fours. Eh? Five six. Well what

72

you playing for? (DEAN *throws*.) Double six.
(*Pause.*)
CONE: First to get three?
DEAN: All right.
(*They go on throwing*.)
FAK: First to get three sixes? Five two. Eh? Six five.
DEAN: Double.
FAK: He's got two now, hasn't he? He's got two
doubles.
CONE: Double.
FAK: Double to you, four two, three dot, two fours.
CONE: Double.
FAK: Equal, two dots, two fives, three dot, four
three.
(*Enter* GRETA, *unnoticed by the others who are
absorbed.*)
PATTY: Hey . . .
(*Pause.*)
GRETA: What you staring at, Yank?
DEAN: I'm wondering whether your hair is natural—
Limey.
CONE: Greta!
GRETA: And what conclusion have you reached?
DEAN: It grows out of your head——
GRETA: Oh yes?
DEAN: And each Friday you dip it in blood—in human
blood.
GRETA: In babies' blood.
DEAN: In cold blood.
CONE: Stop, stop it.
DEAN: Tell me something of yourself, ma'am.
GRETA: I was born in Australia, on the other side of the
world, upside down.
DEAN: Indeed?

73

GRETA: I was reared in a cave by a female wallaby.
Until I was seven I ran about on all fours and
barked. Tell me something of yourself.

DEAN: My childhood was humdrum. I live off cans
and gum.

GRETA: You eat tin?

DEAN: Any kind of sheet metal. I watch so much
television I flicker. What's happening out there?

GRETA: You can get away if you're afraid.

DEAN: I'm not afraid.

GRETA: Well you bloody well should be.

CONE: (*furious*). Kant! Kant! Bloody cow! Go on
gabber! Stand there cool, dead cool, filthy cow!
Filthy cow! Filthy cow!

GRETA: (*silencing* CONE *with howls*). Ow! Ow! Ow!
Ahooer! Ahooer! Ahooer! (*Pause.*) Ah that's
better, anybody got a cigarette?

FAK: What'll we do now?

GRETA: Have a bit of peace.

DEAN: You sure are an extraordinary creature.

GRETA: Break me up and see how I tick.

FAK: Let's get out eh? Let's get after them. A real
scrap, bash 'em off.

GRETA: No. I can't be bothered.

CONE: Why? Why can't you be bothered?

GRETA: Oh buzz.

CONE: Why can't you——

GRETA: Somebody else.

CONE: ——Be bothered? What's the matter? What's the
matter with you?

GRETA: (*at* CONE). Flywheels, gasometers, chimney
stacks, coal dust / newspapers, oranges, broken
glass / stair-carpet, raincoats, geysers /
cigarettes, cinemas. Ah! Ah! / Sausages,

bedsteads, rag and iron merchants / basements,
cement, up and down / Metropolitan, Bakerloo,
Piccadilly / forty-seven, fifty-six, four. Ah! Ah!

DEAN: All flaying claws: ten legs like a lobster.

GRETA: Grab me in the small of the back.

DODO: Blutter the wind, blutter the wind, blutter the
wind—no, it's cold . . .

(DEAN *goes to* DODO.)

CONE: (*going to her wanting to resume their
relationship*). Greta . . . Greta . . .

GRETA: Oh get off. Leave me alone.

FAK: What's happening eh? Shall I do my conjuring
trick?

CONE: Oh, shut up.

FAK: What are we hanging about for? When are our
lot coming? When are we going to do
something?

CONE: Ask her.

FAK: Hey! Hey! Where's our lot? . . . I'm fed up with
this cop. I feel like a skate on a slab and
everybody looking at me . . . why can't she say
something? Why can't she bloody well answer?

CONE: Come over here.

PATTY: What?

CONE: You keep out of this.

FAK: What's the idea?

CONE: (*making sure that* GRETA *can hear*). Notice
anything?

FAK: No, what?

CONE: With——

FAK: With?

CONE: With——

FAK: With her?

CONE: Yes.

75

FAK: What?
CONE: Well?
FAK: Nothing's happening.
CONE: Well?
FAK: She's slipping!
CONE: Well?
FAK: It's that bloody yank—I'll do him.
CONE: You're bright, aren't you?
FAK: What?
CONE: Real bright.
FAK: Oh, I wouldn't say that.
CONE: Seems a pity——
FAK: What?
CONE: A bright chap like you——
FAK: What d'you mean "It's a pity"?
CONE: No chance——
FAK: For what?
CONE: Getting no credit.
FAK: No credit?
CONE: Good looks, intelligence, personality——
FAK: Eh?
CONE: Most popular feller in town.
FAK: Oh, go on!
CONE: (*to audience*). You say so? Yes! He is!
FAK: Cor!
CONE: All you do.
FAK: I do?
CONE: That's right!
FAK: Yes, I do!
CONE: People like you are wanted.
FAK: What for?
CONE: What'll happen now——
FAK: Now?
CONE: To the fellers——

76

FAK: Eh?

CONE: Now she's——

FAK: Now she's——

CONE: Now she's——

FAK: Now she's washed up? That's it! Let's get at the yank!

CONE: Someone with guns, brains, personality . . .

FAK: You mean?

CONE: Well?

FAK: You mean I could be . . .

CONE: You could be.

FAK: King of the Teds!

CONE: King of the Teds!

FAK: King of the Teds!

CONE: (*to the audience*). Meet the King of the Teds! . . . The King of the Teds . . . who else is as sensational, as strong, as stupid.

FAK: Tony Curtis the second.

CONE: All the fellers who've had a bash. All the fellers with cigars and girls and gats.

FAK: King! King! King Fak! I'll put bloody south London in fear of Fak—I'll—I'll——

CONE: Look.

FAK: What?

CONE: That.

FAK: Her?

CONE: Get outside.

FAK: I get outside.

CONE: Find one of them.

FAK: I find one of them.

CONE: Tell 'em she's here.

FAK: I tell 'em she's here . . . tell them she's here?

CONE: They'll break the place to get her and then they'll break her and that'll be that about that.

FAK: I get outside, I find one of them . . . I tell him she's here . . . (*his knees knocking*) what? . . . What?

CONE: What's the matter?

FAK: 'Fraid of what she'll do.

CONE: What'll she do when she hears all this?

FAK: What?

CONE: When I tell——

FAK: You tell her? . . . What? . . . But you won't, you——

CONE: Won't I?

FAK: What are you going to do?

CONE: What do you think?

FAK: Wait.

CONE: No waits.

FAK: I'll—I'll——

CONE: What.

FAK: Go.

CONE: Good.

PATTY: I heard every word you said! Every—you should be ashamed of yourself—and you! What d'you think you're doing? What'll you get from her? What'll you get from him?

FAK: Oh.

CONE: Shut up. Shut up, you silly little bitch.

PATTY: Shut you, you cheeky beast. (*To* FAK) Listen you? You're getting a job, steady. Ten pounds a week regular and furnish on the never-never.

FAK: Ten pounds——

PATTY: Ten pounds regular.

PATTY: And if I keep on at the stores——

FAK: Keep on——

PATTY: We'll go to the flicks and Palais and there'll be television and we might have a bit of garden

and the weeks'll be Monday to Saturday and
we'll have the tele and go dancing sometimes
and we'll never get into debt except on the
never-never but that's different and oh! You'll
do what you're told, what's good for you and
there'll be covers on the chairbacks and table
mats and china condiments and hot water and
electricity. Come on! Before somebody stops us
or hurts us. Let's get off! Let's get off! They're
different! They can stand it—you don't know,
you can't see, but quick! Quick! So I don't
have to see!

CONE: Get off! Get off! You can't hide! They'll find
you! They'll get you.

(*Exit* PATTY *and* FAK.)

Dodo! . . . Soft . . . all looking after
themselves . . . nobody takes any . . . you.
What d'you think you're doing, eh? Garry.
Pampinato. Fak. Fak! What about Fak?—eh?
Fak's splitting—he told me! He's getting you!
He's going to tell Pampi-potato you're here! I
heard him! The Potato'll come and he'll tear!
Tear! After what you did he'll kill you! Take
some notice of me! Take some notice of me!
. . . Somebody do something about me . . .
What does she think she is? . . . What does she
think? . . . Oh, it don't matter to me . . . I'm
not—I'm not taking any . . . bitch! Bitch! Silly
fat bitch! Sow! . . . Sow! . . . Sow! Sow! Sow!
What about me? . . . Stop me! Stop me! Stop
me and buy one! (*Weeping*) All right. All right.
I'm going—I'm going to find him and tell him.
I'll tell him about Ronny and Gerry and
Connie—he'll wreck you. He'll wreck you!

79

Break! Rip! Crack! Tear! And it'll be you! I'll
tell Pampinato and he'll destroy you. The sky'll
be black and purple and the blood'll knot in
the veins and it'll be you! You! I'll destroy
you! I'll destroy earth! I'll destroy everything!
And it'll be you! You! You! You! You!
(CONE *hits* GRETA *like an angry, resentful child
wishing to draw attention to itself but not daring
to hit hard and not having the strength. As he
hits her the quality of his touching changes. He
realizes that she is pregnant. A very long pause.
If possible play without words otherwise add in*
CONE: *You won't want me any more.*
Exit CONE. *Offstage three terrible howls each
farther away in the distance.*)

DEAN: Why did you let Cone go like that?

GRETA: Oh are you still here? What did you say?

DEAN: Why did you let Cone go like that?

GRETA: Well run along, there's a good chap. Just at this
moment I can't be bothered with you.

DEAN: I want to talk to you. No seriously. Someone's
got to talk to you.

GRETA: Here and now? With that lot out there? Are you
crazy? They won't leave us long, you know,
they'll be coming.

DEAN: The fact that they are coming doesn't worry
me.

GRETA: It will, it will.

DEAN: I don't care about dying, or being hurt—or
rather there are things which concern me much
more.

GRETA: You're a drag.

DEAN: We won't talk about me.

GRETA: There's nothing hurts more than being hurt.

80

DEAN: We'll talk about you. Why did you let Cone go?

GRETA: Let's not talk about that now.

DEAN: Yes we will.

GRETA: It's none of your business.

DEAN: The human race is my business.

GRETA: Mr. Big Business.

DEAN: It's not decent. He trusted you, relied on you, lived for you. How can you just turn him off? Don't you see? Strong people have a responsibility towards weak people. If the strong don't help the weak where will it end? It's back to chaos. Looking at it even from the meanest angle of self-interest: if you're a strong person you must help weak people, you must look after old people, for instance. In your own interest you must establish it as a social habit, part of the morals of civilized society that the young and strong protect the weak and old. One day you yourself will be weak and old and then the social law you have made will be your protection.
(GRETA *is in pain.*)
I'm sorry . . . I'm sorry . . . Let me help you . . . is there anything I can do? Let me fetch someone—a doctor—I'm sure I could find a doctor—you ought to be in hospital—let me take you to——

GRETA: No, no not likely, leave me alone . . . go on talking, just go on talking.
(*Pause.*)

DEAN: But that's putting it at its meanest level. There is a far more moral reason why you should protect Cone, why the strong should protect

81

the weak: to act otherwise is below human dignity—don't you see? Every time anyone does anything cruel or immoral—and I don't mean moral in the sexual sense but in its widest sense, moral behaviour in the sense of trying to act with love and truth in all you do—every time anyone does anything cruel or immoral he betrays mankind. I'm not a religious person, at least I'm not a Christian, a churchgoer, but this is what I feel—I can't see any reason for men being on this earth, but since we are here, we men, we must try and become better, we must seek to become better and better, to help to create order, truth and love. It's so easy to slide into chaos—don't you see that? You're intelligent and strong—surely you understand —yes?

GRETA: Eh? What did you say? (*Pause.*) Look, if you don't mind I think I'll toddle along, it's all ever so interesting and thanks ever so but er——

DEAN: I want you to listen to me.

GRETA: Some other time, yes?

DEAN: Stay where you are.

GRETA: Eh?

DEAN: You heard me that time.

GRETA: Fat lot I care.

DEAN: It's obscene, it's obscene. You care nothing for life, for cherishing life, for love, friendship. You're disgusting. Disgusting! Just tearing life down and trampling on it. Reverence for life! Reverence for life! The things you kill can never, never! Be replaced. It's disgusting! It's totally obscene! Agh!

82

GRETA: Oh friend that worries me, that really worries me.

DEAN: I don't care if it worries you! I don't give a damn! You're going to hear. Somebody's got to get it into that thick cruel skull. Don't interrupt me! No self-control! No discipline! What's a world without serenity, without mutual assurance, a bedrock of mutual trust, of laws and decencies you can rely on? Be quiet! All the things decent men have striven for, all the high aims: learning, philosophy, morality, and I don't mean sexual morality, I mean total morality: moral discipline, a moral philosophy of responsibility that each man hammers out for himself and tries to live by.

GRETA: For crying out loud, I'm off——

DEAN: You're not.

GRETA: I am.

(GRETA *starts to go, he pulls her down.*)

DEAN: You're stopping.

GRETA: Rough stuff.

DEAN: Yes.

GRETA: Just you remember it's a pregnant woman you're pulling around.

DEAN: Pregnant! Pregnant woman! You pregnant! You're not fit to have a child. What'll your child be? What'll it's life be?

GRETA: Rough.

DEAN: You're disgusting! You destroy people. You eat them, you eat them. A boy, your friend, trusts you, and you just toss him off: "Go away, I'm sick of you." You obscenity! You gross thing! Man/woman, cruel! Unstable! Frigid!

GRETA : Frigid?

DEAN : Yes frigid! No love, no true morality, no
giving, all taking! You eat men, you eat them,
well, you shan't eat me! You shan't devour me!
You and your kind--how dare you? Look at
me! Look at me! What have you got to say?
What have you got to say? You! You! You!
Dragging us down, down to your level!
Crawling, ferreting among the muck, muck!
And you know what I mean don't you? Muck!
You filthy-minded, vicious! You know it! You
glory in it! Glory! Glory! Glory! Look at me!
Look at me! This is the first time, the first time
you've had it, had it strong and true, and the
first time, yes. And me? I'm telling you, you.
I'm telling—giving it to you straight, straight
and strong. Look at me! You look at me,
straight, straight, at someone giving it you! Yes
sister! Giving it you for the first time—the first
time—and it's me!

(GRETA *in pain which carries forward to her lines
at the end of his speech.*)

Me! I'm the one that's giving it you! D'you
hear? Me! Straight and strong you're getting it,
getting for the first and it's me that's giving it
you, me giving it straight and strong——

GRETA : Strong--strong.

DEAN : Yes strong——

GRETA : But them—the fight—the bash——

DEAN : Bash—bash—lash——

GRETA : Lash——

DEAN : Whiplash! Whiplash! Whiplash and suck,
suck—sucks you down.

GRETA : Sucks down——

84

DEAN: Down—running loose——

GRETA: Running loose—hah hah!

DEAN: Come with me! Come! Come!

GRETA: Lash!

DEAN: Come! Come with me!

GRETA: Lash! Lash!

DEAN: You're coming! You're coming with me if I have to knock you out, knock knock! I just don't care—I just don't—I'll kill—kill——

GRETA: Lash!

DEAN: Kill—It's going to kill——

GRETA: Lash!

DEAN: Kill you kill——

GRETA: Kill——

DEAN: Kill——

GRETA: Bang! I'm dying, I'm in the throes of death! Bang! Bang! Feel! Feel! Bang! Bang! (*Holding* DEAN *by the hair.*) Try and beat me! Try and eat me! Hah! Look at you! You're so weak you can't stand, you'll fall, you're falling. You can't come you can't go. What are you? A whisp of will, a thread of pride, a sigh of thought.

DEAN: Dodo! Dodo! Help me!
(DODO *runs away and exits.*)
The gun! Where's the gun?

GRETA: You want to kill me? Not likely, I'm not going to die before I have to.

DEAN: It's for me, it's for me.

GRETA: Oh go and get rid of yourself, I want to settle with this bastard.
(*An explosion off.*)
Listen! Listen you! Cocky! Pipe down! Listen quick—no no be quiet a minute . . . a moment

—just a moment—oh. This interlocking,
intertwining, interliving—friendship? Love?
Huh! Oh bloody organic confusion . . . Oh
you! Oh you! Oh . . . Oh . . . Oh . . . just here
. . . (*Pause.*) . . . (*Pause.*) . . . (*A long pause.*)
. . . Now I let this child into life. . . . Now I
thrust this bird into the air . . .
(*Machine-gun fire off. Enter* FAK *carrying a large
white sheet and* PATTY *sketchily dressed up as a
nurse and carrying a large book entitled "How
To Deliver A Baby".* STEVE *rams a wig on his
head, picks up a banjo, which he holds like a
tommy-gun, and comes on raking the auditorium
with his "gun".*)

STEVE : (*to audience*). Stay where you are. This is a
stick-up. O.K. where is she?

GRETA : Pampinato!

STEVE : My aboriginee love! Little one, why did you
never tell?

GRETA : I've been a fool, a fool, is it too late?

STEVE : Never say those words "too late". (*To audience*)
One cheep out of you lot and I'll flash you.
(FAK *and* PATTY *hold up the sheet and* GRETA
goes behind.)
What are you doing behind there?

GRETA : What do you think? Lucky you came in time.

STEVE : But you can't do that! It's not nice, not
customary, not legal.

GRETA : Rails, rules, laws, guides, promises, terms,
guarantees, conventions, traditions: into the pot
with the whole bloody lot. Birth! Birth! That's
the thing! Oh, I shall have hundreds of
children, millions of hundreds and hundreds of
millions.

86

STEVE: We'll see about that.

FAK: (*to* PATTY). And shall we be happy, very, very happy?

PATTY: Ooh! You should just see what it says here.

FAK: But they grow under gooseberry bushes . . . don't they?

(*Infant cries from behind the sheet. Sheet falls to reveal* GRETA *and a small white bundle.*)

STEVE: It might be mine, it looks like me . . . it must be mine.

(*A distant cry. Pause.*)

GRETA: What happened to Cone?

FAK: Dead.

GRETA: How did he die?

FAK: He bashed himself to death with a brick. He rubbed himself out.

(*Pause.* DEAN *rises and looks at* GRETA. *Exit* DEAN.)

STEVE: (*to audience*). O.K. you lot, clear out. I'm blowing this place up. We'll have a bonfire: bring your own axes. All right everyone off! Off! (*To* GRETA) And you keep out of mischief—or else . . .

(*Exit* STEVE, FAK *and* PATTY. GRETA *examines the "baby" with lively interest.*)

(*Slow fade.*)

(*The End*)